BEAT AN
IRS
AUDIT

Everything You Need to Know to Avoid, Prepare for, Handle and Beat an IRS Audit

BEAT AN
IRS
AUDIT

Everything You Need to Know to Avoid, Prepare for, Handle and Beat an IRS Audit

JAMES O. PARKER
ATTORNEY AT LAW

SPHINX® PUBLISHING
AN IMPRINT OF SOURCEBOOKS, INC.®
NAPERVILLE, ILLINOIS
www.SphinxLegal.com

AUG 1 0 2007

First Edition: 2007

Published by: Sphinx® Publishing, An Imprint of Sourcebooks, Inc.®

Naperville Office
P.O. Box 4410
Naperville, Illinois 60567-4410
630-961-3900
Fax: 630-961-2168
www.sourcebooks.com
www.SphinxLegal.com

This publication is designed to provide accurate and authoritative information in regard to the subject matter covered. It is sold with the understanding that the publisher is not engaged in rendering legal, accounting, or other professional service. If legal advice or other expert assistance is required, the services of a competent professional person should be sought.

From a Declaration of Principles Jointly Adopted by a Committee of the American Bar Association and a Committee of Publishers and Associations

This product is not a substitute for legal advice.

Disclaimer required by Texas statutes.

Library of Congress Cataloging-in-Publication Data

Parker, James O., 1948-
  Beat an IRS audit : everything you need to know to avoid, prepare for,
handle and beat an IRS audit / by James O. Parker. -- 1st ed.
     p. cm.
  ISBN-13: 978-1-57248-579-2 (pbk. : alk. paper)
  ISBN-10: 1-57248-579-5 (pbk. : alk. paper)
  1. Tax auditing--United States--Popular works. 2. United States. Internal
Revenue Service--Popular works. I. Title.

KF6314.Z9P37 2007
343.7304--dc22

2006101804

Printed and bound in the United States of America.
SB — 10 9 8 7 6 5 4 3 2 1

Contents

**Chapter Four: Federal Income Taxes and
                    Common Tax Credits** **61**
Regular Federal Income Taxes
Alternative Minimum Tax
Self-Employment Taxes
Tax Credits

SECTION II: AUDIT ESSENTIALS **67**

Chapter Five: The Audit Process **69**
The Letter Audit
The Office Audit
The Field Audit

Chapter Six: IRS Approaches to Audits **81**
The Bank Deposits Method
Indirect Methods of Establishing Income—
     Using Earnings to Reconstruct Income
Indirect Methods of Establishing Income—
     Using Expenditures Plus Increase in
     Net Worth to Determine Income
The IRS Response to the Cash Hoard Defense

**Chapter Seven: Circumstances that are
                    Most Likely to Cause an Audit** **91**
Income From Self-employment
Using the Services of Independent Contractors
Owning an Interest in a Partnership or Small Business
A Dealer Showing Investment Income in the
     Items in Which He or She Deals
     Securities Dealers
     Real Estate Dealers
     Royalty Income
Deducting Business Losses
     Combining Activities in Order to
          Qualify for the Presumption
     Proving a Profit Motive When the
          Presumption Does Not Apply
Taking a Deduction for an In-Home Office

Introduction

During the course of a series of radio talk show interviews in connection with two of my other books, *Tax Smarts for Small Business* and *Tax Power for the Self-Employed*, the most common questions that arose pertained to IRS audits. Almost without fail, taxpayers who receive notice from the IRS that they have been selected for audit feel somewhat panic-stricken over it. With the IRS having announced that it intends to step up its enforcement efforts, which is another way of saying that it intends to increase the number of taxpayers that it audits, and the uneasiness that people feel over the prospect of being audited, it was apparent that it was a good time to write a book of practical advice to taxpayers on the subject of tax audits.

Beat an IRS Audit deals in some detail with three broad aspects of dealing with IRS audits. Ideally, taxpayers should start preparing for an audit from the very first moment that they have income and incur tax deductions. The first section of the book, which is comprised of the first four chapters, provides a basic look at what constitutes income for tax purposes in the U.S., what expenses and allowances are tax deductible, the tax impact of those deductible expenses and allowances, and the types of taxes that are commonly imposed on typical taxpayers. Attention is focused on common trouble spots that tend to draw the attention of the IRS for purposes of audits. The purpose of this segment is to put taxpayers on notice concerning practices that might result in an audit, as well as arming them with the information that they need in order to document the proof that they would likely need in order to successfully respond to an IRS audit if they are chosen for one.

The second section of *Beat an IRS Audit* focuses primarily on the IRS audit process. The different types of audit processes are explained in an easy-to-understand manner so that a taxpayer will know what to expect from each. A chapter is devoted to the various approaches that the IRS uses in determining whether or not a taxpayer has filed a federal tax return that has understated his or her taxable income. The section concludes with a chapter on specific circumstances that are most likely to cause a taxpayer to be chosen for an audit by the IRS.

The third section of *Beat an IRS Audit* is concerned with record-keeping in preparing for the possibility of a future audit by the IRS, as well as instructions for responding to an actual IRS audit notice. The final chapter is devoted to taxpayers who find themselves in the unhappy circumstance of owing a sizable tax deficiency to the U.S. Treasury. By becoming familiar with the various ways in which they may address their tax deficiencies, taxpayers will be equipped to more intelligently deal with tax professionals and the IRS in addressing those deficiencies.

One of the best ways to overcome fear and panic is through knowledge. Understanding how IRS auditors think, how they choose taxpayers for audits, how they go about the business of conducting those audits, and the sort of proof that taxpayers must provide in order to survive a challenge by an auditor gives taxpayers the knowledge that they need to respond to an audit notice with confidence. *Beat an IRS Audit's* prepare-as-you-go approach to dealing with the potential for an IRS audit is designed to help taxpayers achieve such a comfort level with their recordkeeping and tax preparation that an audit notice will be viewed as an opportunity to meet the challenge rather than a cause for panic. Taxpayers who have received an audit notice from the IRS without having previously had the benefit of the guidance offered in this book will still find it useful in preparing for their audits as they set about to gather requested documentation. It will give them the guidance they need in what to expect from the auditor. For those taxpayers who are confronted with large amounts of unpaid taxes, it is hoped that this book's explanations of the ways of dealing with what may seem to be an insurmountable tax delinquency will help them resolve their tax problems.

SECTION I

THE BASICS OF U.S. INCOME TAXATION OF INDIVIDUALS

Chapter One
Income

In order to more fully understand what triggers a tax audit by the Internal Revenue Service, and what an individual auditor may be looking for in the course of an audit, it is necessary to understand the basics of the tax laws that apply to the party being audited. Through the years, Congress has frequently fine-tuned the tax laws by changing tax rates, allowable deductions, and qualifications for and amounts of exemptions and credits. Even though these changes seem frequent (and to some extent arbitrary), the truth is that the basic structure of U.S. tax law has remained in tact for decades.

The primary determinant as to how a particular taxpayer will be taxed is whether the party is an individual, a business entity, or a trust or an estate. This book will focus on the individual (and what that really means under the tax law), with some discussion on businesses to the extent they affect an individual's tax return.

To talk about audits, and more importantly preventing and dealing with them, it is unfortunately necessary to sometimes talk about the tax law, in particular the *Internal Revenue Code* (I.R.C.). While specific code references are sometimes cited, it is not as important that you concern yourself with the actual Code reference number as it is that you understand the concepts behind the Code.

With that in mind, however, specific citations will be used so you can do additional research, should that be necessary, and so you have some familiarity with the terminology you may come across from the IRS on a particular notice or from an auditor assigned to your case. Don't let the lingo scare you—remember that the rule is important, not how it is referred to by the IRS.

Who is an Individual?

You are an individual. You file some version of the 1040 to report to the IRS your tax liability. Married couples who file joint returns (file together on the same 1040 form) are also considered to be individuals for purposes of U.S. tax law. If you and your spouse file separate tax returns, you each are still considered individuals individually, but collectively you are not.

Taxpayers who earn their livelihoods from *self-employment* without having created a formal business entity are also considered individuals. A self-employed person shows all of his or her profit or loss from being self-employed on his or her individual tax return. If you have your own business—big or small—but never created a separate formal business entity, you and that business together are considered an individual. Those types of businesses, referred to as *sole proprietorships*, are not recognized as being separate from the individual owner.

If you have taken steps to formalize your business, such as by incorporating, organizing a *limited liability company* (LLC), or forming a partnership, that business is now considered separate from you and must be treated such as when dealing with the IRS. A taxpayer who has formed a corporation or a limited liability company, for example, must file a return for that entity, even if he or she is the sole owner of the company, as well as an individual return for him- or herself.

It is already sounding complicated, but you are probably more aware of this than you may think. If you are not running your own business, then these additional returns are not even applicable to your situation, so there is nothing to worry about. If you are self-employed, you have probably already filed a few returns before and know all about this. If you are reading this because you are thinking about starting your own business and have heard people who file returns with self-employment income get audited more than others—you are right and you should pay particular attention. Keep reading and everything will be made clear.

Income of Individuals

Individuals who earn a certain amount of income (the amount is low, so it probably includes you) must prepare and file an income tax return reporting the income they earned. Again, this is nothing new, but the problems begin with the questions of what the IRS considers income and when it is considered to have been received.

It is important to understand what the IRS considers, because failure to understand often results in an audit being initiated. Not all money you receive is income, but what is more troublesome is that how you receive the money—meaning where the money is coming from and why you are receiving it—is what determines how you are to claim it on your return. Classifying money received the wrong way can have dramatic affects on how that money is taxed, and if you get it wrong—or classify it differently than the IRS—an audit can occur.

A large part of the rest of this chapter will look at several different things that qualify as income, and specifically are consid-ered *gross income* by the IRS. *Gross income* is the starting point for your income tax burden calculation. For most people, these items will also be defined as ordinary income by the IRS, which really means nothing more than they have determined that the money you received will be taxed at the ordinary, as opposed to special, rates. For now, just think about income received as wages, salary, or commission by an employee or generated from a self-employed person's trade or business as ordinary income. You do a job, you get paid, you have earned income.

In addition, interest acquired on money loaned, gains on assets sold that were held for a year or less prior to sale, and rental income received from allowing another party to use or occupy realty or personal property is also ordinary income. So if you loan someone money and earn interest, sell a short-term investment, or rent out something you own, you have earned ordinary income.

Before looking at all the subclassifications the IRS has of income, the second part of the question previously discussed— when income is considered to have been received—should be addressed. The IRS makes this determination through a concept called *realization*. This is a fancy word that boils down to the idea that you actually must have the income in your hands to be forced to claim it. Don't take that as a literal definition, as there are plenty of times (that will be discussed) when you will be deemed to have realized some income, when you in fact did not actually see a dime of it—but for the most part, this working definition helps explain the concept.

To realize income, some event must occur that converts *potential income*, such as appreciation in the value of an asset, into *actual gain*. It is at that moment that the income resulting from the occurrence is considered to be realized and the tax consequences will result. Among the events that can result in realization of income are money you earn (when you get paid for some work you do), a sale or exchange of an asset, destruction or theft of an asset (very complicated and discussed much later), or completion of work to the degree necessary to entitle a worker to be paid.

EXAMPLE:
Linda bought a piece of real estate for $190,000. The property was located on a major highway, and within three years, development in the area pushed prices up to the point that she had an offer from a developer to buy the property for $550,000. She refused to sell the property. Despite the fact that she had a bona fide offer from a ready, willing, and able buyer, which clearly established that the property had appreciated $360,000, she will have no taxable income. Without an actual sale of the property, she will not have access to the gain, and therefore, the gain will not be considered to be realized.

As stated, the idea of realization is a little more complicated than whether you got paid or not. There are instances when you could receive money and it still not be considered income under U.S. tax law, as well as times when you did not receive payment and are still considered to have been paid under the law. For example, money that a student receives from his or her parents may be regarded by the recipient as income, but since gifts are not considered to be income under U.S. law (see p. 17), if no goods or work were exchanged for the allowance, no income tax will be imposed upon the recipient. Conversely,

AUDIT ALERT

If you postpone recognition of available income, IRS auditors, upon detection of the failure to recognize income, will consider that income to have been constructively received and will recalculate your tax liabilities accordingly.

there are also instances in which a party will be considered to have earned income that he or she has not actually received. Once a taxpayer has done everything necessary in order to be entitled to payment for work performed, and the payment is available, the income is considered to have been realized, and subject to taxation. If the money is available to you and you postpone receipt of the payment in hopes to cause the income to be taxed in a later year, if audited, the IRS will consider you to have received the income when payment was available, regardless of when you actually received it. In short, you pay taxes on the income you earn (not gifts) when you earn it, whether you took payment or not.

EXAMPLE:

During the course of the year, Reed, a self-employed contractor, had completed and been paid for an unusually involved project. Fearing that another sizable payment would push him into a higher tax bracket, when a client presented him with a check at the conclusion of a project in late December, Reed refused to take the check and told the client to mail it to him on the 31st of December. Although Reed will not actually take physical possession of the check until January of the following year, he will be considered to have realized the income when it became available to him in the preceding December, and if he is taxed on a calendar-year basis, he will be required to report the income in the year in which he realized it rather than in the year in which he actually received it.

The IRS term for when a party postpones receiving payment at the time he or she could have is called *constructive receipt*. If you postpone recognition of available income, IRS auditors, upon detection of the failure to recognize income, will consider that income to have been constructively received and will recalculate your tax liabilities accordingly. They will also add penalties and interest for your failure to make the appropriate payment when due.

Receiving *something* can result in receiving income, but what is that "something"? The following several sections discuss that something and provide clarity.

Earnings from Employment

For most people, the primary source of their income that is subject to taxation is the money they earn from working. Some tax protesters have argued that they are merely trading their labor for money and that, unlike the profit made when goods are sold for a higher price than was paid for them, there is no profit made from the trade of labor for money, and consequently, their income should not be taxed. However, such protesters have lost every court case based on this argument, and payments for work performed— whether those payments are labeled as salary, wages, bonuses, commissions, or some other income, or whether they result from self-employment—are considered to be taxable income.

In order to police taxpayers and make sure they report the earnings they receive from employers, the Internal Revenue Code requires that employers furnish W-2 forms, which report an individual worker's earnings and taxes withheld, to each employee and to the IRS. If a worker's tax return fails to include the full amount of earnings reported to him or her on Form W-2, it will result in an audit or some form of inquiry from the IRS.

Self-employed workers do not get W-2 forms for the self-employed work they do.

AUDIT ALERT

If a worker's tax return fails to include the full amount of earnings reported to him or her on Form W-2, it will result in an audit or some form of inquiry from the IRS.

Instead, if they perform services as independent contractors for companies, the Internal Revenue Code requires that the amount of the payment that they receive for such work be reported to both the worker and the IRS on a Form 1099. If a self-employed worker fails to report gross revenue equal to at least as much as the combined total on the 1099 forms that he or she received, that taxpayer will be subjected to some form of audit.

Interest

Interest, which is money received by a party for letting someone else use his or her money, is included in I.R.C. §61(a)(4) as a source of gross income unless it is specifically excluded from taxation by statute, as is interest received on debt obligations of states and their political subdivisions. If you loan money to someone, the IRS says you must collect interest on that loaned money, and then report it as income.

Other than outright failure to report *interest income*, IRS auditors are more likely to concern themselves with imputed interest. Whenever taxpayers lend money that is to be paid back at some future time, or sell goods that are to be paid for at a future time, and do not specify that the borrower is to pay interest, the IRS will impute interest on the transaction. As a result, part of the proceeds collected by the lender or creditor will be re-characterized as interest and taxed accordingly. Interest will also be imputed on interest-free loans that are never repaid because the lender forgives the indebtedness, making them a gift. When interest is imputed, the *applicable federal rate*, which is the rate paid by the federal government on funds that it borrows for a similar period, is used. The rates are calculated monthly and include a short-term rate for loans of three years or less, a mid-term rate for loans of over three years but not over nine years, and a long-term rate for loans with a duration in excess of nine years.

EXAMPLE:

Clem wanted to retire, sell his home in the city, and move to a small cabin in the Ozark Mountains. He and his wife, Zelda, planned on using the proceeds from the sale of their home to generate income to supplement their pensions. They lived in the home, which they bought for $50,000, for many years, and meet IRS requirements to exclude the gain from the sale as income. They could sell the house for $240,000, which would generate only about $800 a month in income, if invested at the prevailing 4% rate for certificates of deposit, and that income would then be subject to federal income tax. The buyer approached Clem about selling the house to him through owner financing. Clem agreed, but only if the sale price were shown to be $500,000 payable at $3,333 per month for 15 years at a zero interest rate. This is approximately equivalent to Clem selling his $240,000 home at its fair market value and financing the entire sale price at 15% interest. By structuring the transaction as a $500,000 sale with owner financing at zero interest, Clem figures that he can exclude from federal taxation the entire total of the payments that he receives, since his gain would not exceed $500,000 and is from the sale of a qualified primary residence. However, were Clem to be audited, the IRS would re-characterize part of the payments received by him as interest, which would be subject to federal taxation.

Rents

For federal tax purposes, the term *rents* refers to money received for letting someone else use the recipient's real estate or personal property. Only the net income from the rental of property is included in a taxpayer's gross income to the degree that deductions are allowed for expenses, such as maintenance, taxes, insurance, advertising, and repairs associated with rental activities, as well as depreciation of the rental property. When taxpayers with rental income are audited, there is usually little dispute over the amount of the rental income received, since it is typically deposited in a bank account and is readily verifiable. However, disputes over the deductibility of expenses by landlords are common.

In order to qualify for a deduction from rental income, an expense must be *ordinary and necessary*, a concept discussed subsequently in the section on business deductions. (see Chapter 2.) In addition to reviewing rental-related deductions to verify that they were ordinary and necessary, IRS auditors also check to make sure that taxpayers are not improperly including their personal expenses among their rental expense deductions.

Royalties

Payments for the right to use property, such as written materials, patents, trademarks, and formulas, are referred to as *royalties*, as are payments for the right to exploit natural resources, such as oil, minerals, or timber. Royalties are included in gross income in I.R.C. §61(a)(6) and are regarded as ordinary income.

Dividends

If a corporation that has not elected to be taxed under Subchapter S of the Internal Revenue Code makes a non-liquidating distribution of cash or property from either current or accumulated earnings and profits, it constitutes a dividend and is includible in the recipient's gross income under the provisions of I.R.C. §61(a)(7). If you own stock from a company that pays you a dividend, you have received income. As long as you claim it as such, there is little audit potential.

Where audit potential increases is when a corporation makes what is called a *nimble dividend*. This will usually only occur from a privately held corporation, such as a family business. When a nimble dividend is granted, it is not being done through the corporation's earnings and profits. As such, the payment will be viewed as merely a return of capital.

Rather than being included in the recipient's gross income, nimble dividends merely reduce the party's adjusted basis in the stock for which the dividend was paid. Therefore, when a stockholder who has received a nimble dividend sells his or her stock, rather than calculating gains and losses on the transaction by subtracting the actual purchase price of the stock from its sale price, the party must reduce the purchase price by the nimble dividend and subtract the remainder from the sale price. The result will be that taxpayers who have received nimble dividends will experience larger gains or smaller losses, as the case may be, when they sell their stock.

Once a recipient's adjusted basis in a company's stock is reduced to zero, any further nimble dividends paid by the company will be classified as capital gains. As a return of basis or as a capital gain, the nimble dividend is not ordinary income, and therefore, is taxed at a lower rate than other income. This can trigger an audit, since special treatment is being made for the payment of the dividends.

Distributive Share of Partnership Income

Internal Revenue Code §61(a)(13) provides that a partner's distributive share of partnership gross income shall be included in his or her gross income. Partnerships and entities that are taxed as partnerships, such as eligible corporations whose owners have elected to be taxed under provisions of Subchapter S of

AUDIT ALERT

IRS auditors concern themselves with *imputed interest*.

the Internal Revenue Code (S corporations), must file annual tax returns, but do not incur tax liabilities. Such organizations show their income on their tax returns and then further show each partner's distributive share of the organization's income or loss. Each owner's distributive share of income from such organizations will be reported to him or her and to the IRS, and must be included in his or her gross income regardless of whether or not he or she actually received a distribution.

If such an organization were to have income, as shown on its tax return, but were to have used the money to acquire inventory, buy equipment, or simply have retained the money to meet future needs, these would be common instances in which a partner would have taxable income to report without having actually received it. Failure to report such income, which is commonly referred to as *phantom income*, will most assuredly result in action by the IRS. This happens because a copy of the Form K-1, which is the form that partnerships and entities that are taxed as partnerships send to owners to report their share of company income to them, will also be provided to the IRS. If the taxpayer's income that is reported on his or her tax return does not match what is reported on the Form K-1, some type of audit will be triggered.

Income from Discharge of Indebtedness

Although funds received as proceeds of a loan are not considered to be income, there are a number of situations involving loans that can result in the realization of taxable income. There are instances in which taxpayers have attempted to escape taxation by characterizing payments that they were to receive as if they were loans, although they were not actually obligated to ever repay the money. To the degree that these sham loans are really payments for goods or services,

AUDIT ALERT

Disputes over the deductibility of expenses by landlords are common and often lead to an audit.

they will be re-characterized appropriately as income, and penalties and interest will be assessed on top of tax liabilities when there is a resulting tax deficiency. If nothing is given in exchange for the sham loan, it will be re-characterized as a gift, which will not result in any income tax liability to the recipient, but may generate a gift tax liability for the donor.

Even when loans are originally bona fide legal obligations that the borrowers intend to repay, there can still be realization of taxable income to the debtor in the event that the debt is forgiven or cancelled. Unless it can be shown that the cancelled amount of a debt was a gift, I.R.C. §61(a)(12) provides that the cancelled amount will be regarded as income to the debtor. Income due to cancellation of debt can arise whether the debt is entirely or only partially cancelled, unless the party whose debt was cancelled was either insolvent or bankrupt. A debt that is owed to a corporation by one of its stockholders that is forgiven will be regarded as a dividend to the stockholder. Otherwise, cancelled debt is generally treated as ordinary income.

Other Section 61 Sources of Gross Income

There are a number of other types of income specifically listed in I.R.C. §61 that are includible in gross income for tax purposes. Among them is pension income (to the extent that it exceeds the recipient's contributions to the fund from previously taxed earnings), income from life insurance (although most death benefits are excluded under I.R.C. §101), and gross income from endowment contracts (which are agreements in which participants pay money to another party for future payments, usually in anticipation of retirement).

In addition to the relatively traditional sources of gross income, I.R.C. §61 also specifically provides for inclusion in

AUDIT ALERT

Your audit potential increases when a corporation makes what is called a *nimble dividend* to you.

gross income of payments received for alimony or separate maintenance. By requiring the recipients of alimony and payments for
separate maintenance to report the receipts as gross income, the
incidence of taxation is shifted from the party paying it to the recipient, since the paying party is allowed a deduction for the payments.
In order to be eligible to take a deduction for alimony payments
that a taxpayer has made, he or she must provide the IRS with the
recipient's Social Security number on the very line on which the
deduction is taken. Therefore, the IRS will have a way to verify
whether the recipient has properly reported alimony receipts, and
if the recipient's tax return does not include the amount of income
that was reported as paid to the party, that will trigger some form
of IRS audit of both the party who claims to have paid alimony, and
the party who is alleged to have received it.

Still another provision of I.R.C. §61 requires that *income in
respect of a decedent* be included in gross income. Such income
arises when a taxpayer who is entitled to income that is taxable
dies before he or she receives it. In such cases, the income must
be included in the gross income of the party who acquires the
right to receive the income as reported on a Form W-2.

Audit Alert

If the alimony recipient's tax return does not include the amount of income that was reported as paid to the party, that will trigger some form of IRS audit of both the party who claims to have paid alimony, as well as the party who is alleged to have received it.

Gross Income

Section 61 of the Internal Revenue Code defines *gross income* to include both ordinary income and income other than ordinary income. In order to determine a taxpayer's tax liability, start with gross income, which is then reduced by any allowable deductions and exemptions before applying the appropriate tax rates in order to arrive at the amount of tax that will be assessed. Whether a particular source of revenue is includible in gross income is a matter of legislative decree, as set forth in I.R.C. §61, and the legislature's decision to include or exclude receipts from its definition of gross income is not always logical. Many of the types of income that are included in gross income have already been discussed. However, it is as important to understand what is not included in gross income as it is to understand what is included.

Income Excluded From Taxation

There are a number of sources of income that, due to legislative grace, are not regarded as gross income to the recipient. Your first thought may be, "Why worry about any of these provisions, since if they are not included in income, I have no audit worries?" Unfortunately, any benefit from the IRS usually comes with a price, and the price is often strict compliance with the rules. Failure to follow the rules the IRS has set up can cause you to believe something should be excluded from the calculations of your gross income, when in fact an auditor will add it to your tax burden.

Among the most important statutory exclusions from gross income are gifts and inheritances, most insurance proceeds, some disability income, the part of the proceeds from sale of assets that represents recovery of adjusted basis, and much of the gain from the sale of primary residences.

Gifts and Inheritances

Money or property received by taxpayers as a gift will not be subject to income tax. Under the provisions of I.R.C. §102, it does not matter whether the gift is made while the donor is living, known as an *inter vivos gift*, or inherited from a deceased donor as a *testamentary gift*.

Either way, it is not considered as part of the recipient's gross income (not to be confused with the possible gift tax burden imposed on a living donor or estate tax to a deceased party's estate).

Since gifts are tax-free to the recipient, taxpayers are often tempted to disguise wages, salaries, and other forms of compensation as gifts in order to avoid taxation of them. Such schemes usually involve one party providing goods or services to another party as a "gift," but the recipient is expected to reciprocate with an appropriate "gift." This trading of goods and services is often referred to by the IRS as *bartering* and has long been an activity that attracts the interest of IRS auditors.

Even if money or property was acquired by inheritance, it will not be excluded from federal income taxation if the funds came from earned income of the deceased that had not been previously taxed, such as accrued wages or an individual retirement account. Employers and financial institutions that make such distributions will report them to the IRS on a Form W-2 or Form 1099 so the IRS can verify that the recipient properly reports them.

Insurance Proceeds

Most insurance proceeds are not subject to federal income taxation unless they replace wages or cause a taxpayer to realize a gain on an asset that is damaged, destroyed, or stolen. You may wonder how you can have a gain from something that is damaged, destroyed, or stolen. It can actually occur a couple of different ways. A gain can result from an insurance settlement when the insurance proceeds received for a loss exceed what the taxpayer paid for the asset. Insurance companies generally try to make sure this doesn't happen, but if you took depreciation on an item that appreciated in value, it is certainly possible.

AUDIT ALERT

The trading of goods and services is often referred to by the IRS as *bartering*, and has long been an activity that attracts the interest of IRS auditors.

Gains are more common when the insured receives an insurance payment that was less than the cost of the damaged property, but the insured has depreciated the property and must recognize the difference between the insurance settlement and the cost of the property, less depreciation, as a taxable gain. This is more common than you may think, especially with people who have business- related property that they have depreciated as a business expense, that is damaged, destroyed, or stolen.

Insurance proceeds paid to an injured party to cover the costs of medical care or as compensation for pain and suffering will not be considered as taxable income. However, insurance payments to replace income lost while recuperating from an injury are considered to be part of the recipient's gross income, unless they are received under provisions of a no-fault car insurance policy or an accident or health insurance policy for which the recipient had paid the premiums with after-tax earnings.

Whether income paid to a recipient to replace work income lost due to illness or disability, referred to as *disability income*, is subject to inclusion in gross income depends on whether it was the recipient or the employer that bore the cost of obtaining the benefit. Section 105 of the I.R.C. provides that if a party's employer pays the premium for a recipient's disability income policy or makes contributions into a fund from which benefits are to be paid, any benefits collected from such sources are fully includible in the recipient's gross income. However, if a recipient pays premiums for his or her disability income policy or makes the contributions to a disability income fund from his or her own after-tax funds, or is taxed on such payments made on his or her behalf by his or her employer, any disability income payments that he or she receives from those sources will be excluded from his or her gross income.

The taxability of many forms of insurance proceeds depends on whether the premiums were written off as a tax deduction or paid with after-tax dollars. Therefore, it is important that taxpayers maintain proof of when premiums are paid with previously taxed funds so they can establish the nontaxable status of their insurance proceeds in the event of an audit.

Recovery of Adjusted Basis from the Sale of an Asset

To the degree that a taxpayer sells or otherwise disposes of assets and merely recovers the amount invested (basis) in the property, there will be no tax consequences from that transaction. Section 1001 of the Internal Revenue Code provides that only the gain from the sale of goods shall be included in a taxpayer's gross income. The part of the proceeds from such a sale that constitutes the seller's adjusted basis in the property is what is viewed as his or her investment in it, and that portion of his or her proceeds is not included in his or her gross income. Taxpayers who overstate the amount they pay for the goods they sell or the investments they make will understate their incomes. This is why auditors will demand substantiation of those expenditures by taxpayers who have made such payments and have been selected for an audit.

Gain from a Primary Residence

The U.S. Tax Code provides one of its greatest benefits to homeowners who realize gains upon the sale of their homes. Section 121 permits married homeowners who file joint returns to exclude up to $500,000 of gain from sale of their primary residence from their gross incomes. Those whose filing status is something other than married filing jointly may exclude only $250,000 of gain from the sale of their primary residence. Generally, in order to qualify for the exclusion provided for in §121, a taxpayer must have occupied the property as his or her principal residence for at least two of the last five years and cannot have taken the exclusion for another primary residence during the last two years.

What makes §121 especially beneficial to taxpayers is that, unlike past laws that merely deferred gain on the sale of a primary residence, it actually permanently excludes such gain from taxation. Furthermore, there is no requirement that a party excluding gain under §121 reinvest the proceeds in the purchase of another primary residence. There is also no limit to how many sales the party may take the exclusion on, as long as he or she meets the holding period requirement and the property that he or she sold was his or her principal residence.

The date of acquisition of a property, as well as the date of its sale, are generally a matter of public record and are not open to debate. However, in the event of an audit, a taxpayer who has excluded the gain from the sale of a residence may be prevailed upon to prove that the property met all of the statutory requirements to be considered a residence for purposes of §121. Treasury Regulation §1.121-1(b) further clarifies this, and states that whether a property should be considered to be a party's residence "depends on all the facts and circumstances." It further states that houseboats and house trailers can be a principal residence if they otherwise qualify. For those who spend time residing in more than one residence, the regulation provides that the principal residence will be the one used by the taxpayer for the majority of the time, and looks at the party's place of employment, place of family member's residence, address listed on tax returns and other government-related documents (such as voter registration and driver's license), location of the party's bank, and party's mailing address in determining his or her principal place of residence.

Since there is a possibility that a taxpayer's gain from the sale of a residence may not

AUDIT ALERT

Taxpayers who overstate the amount they pay for the goods they sell or the investments they make will understate their incomes, and auditors will demand substantiation of those expenditures during an audit.

qualify for exclusion under §121, or with real estate values escalating as rapidly as they are in some areas, a taxpayer's gain may exceed the excludable maximum, it is strongly recommended that homeowners keep good records that establish their basis in their properties. The determination of basis for real estate generally starts with its purchase price and is then increased by any amount spent on permanent improvements. Basis is decreased by deductions taken for use as a home office, depreciation for periods in which it, or part of it, was rented out, and insurance proceeds collected for damage or destruction to the extent that they were not used for repairs or replacement.

Since proceeds from the sale of a property are not taxed to the extent that they are merely a recovery of basis, even if the sale does not qualify for exclusion as a primary residence, it is advisable for taxpayers to fully include all of their qualified expenditures in the basis of their properties. You should maintain records that prove those expenditures, in order to minimize any gains you have that might be taxable.

Assigning Income

The last part involving income that frequently gets certain taxpayers into audit troubles is when taxpayers attempt to evade taxation of their income by assigning their right to receive income to someone else. Typically, this practice involves a taxpayer who is in a relatively high marginal tax bracket causing his or her own income to be paid to someone else, who is in a relatively low tax bracket. The income is then treated by the two individuals involved, for tax purposes, as if it had been earned by the recipient rather than the party who actually earned it. The result is that the income is taxed at a lower rate than it would be had the income been properly reported by the party who earned it, or it may escape taxation altogether.

EXAMPLE:
John, a self-employed lobbyist, did a consulting job for a medical provider seeking a state contract. When it came time to collect his fee of $5,000, John had the company write the check to his daughter, Latisha, who is a college student and does not have a job. As a result of his assigning the $5,000 fee to Latisha, John plans on excluding the income from his taxable earnings and having Latisha report the income on her tax return. If Latisha had no other income, her reported earnings would be so low that she would pay no federal income tax on the earnings that were assigned to her. However, since Latisha did not perform work to earn the fee, the IRS would consider John to have constructively received the $5,000, and then made a gift of it to his daughter.

John's scheme in the previous example would be illegal, and if detected, would certainly result in penalties and interest, and could even result in criminal prosecution. John could have legally achieved the same result by hiring his daughter to work for him and paying her a salary. The salary that he pays his daughter for the work that she does will be a deductible expense for him that will offset his taxable income, and will be taxable income for his daughter. However, in order for John to be entitled to a legitimate salary deduction for payments to his daughter, she must actually provide services for her compensation, and her rate of pay must be commensurate with the type of work that she does in light of her levels of skill, work experience, and education.

In addition to the deliberate attempts to assign income and escape taxation, there are also instances in which taxpayers assign income without realizing that they have done so. This is particularly common in situations involving the purchase of a business by means of payments to the seller out of future earnings. Under this scenario, a certain percentage of business earnings are to be paid to the former owner of the business in order to complete the purchase. What tends to happen is the buyer treats these payments to the former owner as if they were a salary, which is taxable to the recipient, but deductible as a salary expense by the party that paid him or her. However, it is inappropriate to characterize the payments in such a manner.

Payments from profits by a buyer to a seller for payment for a business will be first treated by the IRS as income to the new owner, from which payments are then made to the former owner, and upon detection of such an arrangement, the IRS will regard such payments that are made directly from a new owner to a former owner as having initially been constructively received by the new owner. The result will be additional income from his or her business to the buyer and proceeds from the sale of the business to the seller, rather than earned income for the seller.

EXAMPLE:
Fauzia agreed to sell her dental practice to Spike for $250,000. At the closing of the sale, Spike paid Fauzia $100,000, and agreed to pay the remaining $150,000 by giving Fauzia 20% of his profits each year until the balance was fully paid. At the conclusion of his first year of operation, Spike determined that he had made a profit of $200,000 and wrote a check to Fauzia for $40,000, which he deducted as a labor expense, and he sent a form to the IRS indicating that Fauzia had been paid $40,000 by his business. Spike's treatment of the $40,000 payment to Fauzia is improper. Spike has essentially assigned $40,000 of his own income to

Fauzia. Proper tax treatment would require Spike to report his full $200,000 profit as income, and Fauzia would be required to report the $40,000 as part of the proceeds from the sale of her dental practice. Spike would not be allowed to deduct the $40,000 as an expense of operating his practice, but would regard it as a part of his investment in the dental practice, known as *basis*, which he will subtract from the proceeds he receives if he ever sells the business in order to determine his gain or loss from the sale.

What often happens in situations similar to the one depicted in the previous example is that, after a few years of receiving payments that are reported to the IRS as salary (when they are actually payments for the purchase of a business), the recipient becomes aware that the payments that he or she has received were not actually salary, but payments for an asset. As a result, those payments should have been subjected to capital gains tax, which is usually no more than 15%, rather than being taxed as earned income, which can be subject to up to a 35% income tax rate, plus either FICA or self-employment taxes. The recipient of the payments will be permitted to file amended returns in order to claim a refund for the overpayment of taxes for as far back as the preceding three years, and if he or she does so, the party who made those payments and claimed an improper salary deduction for them will almost certainly then be audited. The result will be disallowance of the salary expense deductions for the

AUDIT ALERT

If you bought a business and plan to pay for it by making payments to the seller from your profits, the IRS will treat the payments as income to you even if they are made directly to the seller.

payments to the seller of the business, which will result in an increase in the buyer's tax liability, along with the attendant penalties and interest. When the payments involved have been sizable and multiple years are involved, there is considerable potential for a sizable liability for taxes, interest, and penalties.

Chapter Two
Deductions

Once a taxpayer's gross income is determined, it is reduced by allowable deductions. In tax parlance, this is known as *adjusting your gross income*. The most significant factor in determining the impact of a deduction on a taxpayer's tax liability is whether it is an *above-the-line* deduction or a *below-the-line* deduction. The line referred to in making the determination is the line on tax returns that contains the figure for adjusted gross income.

Calculations of a party's tax liability begin with his or her gross income, which is reduced by above-the-line reductions to yield adjusted gross income. Below-the-line deductions are then subtracted from the taxpayer's adjusted gross income as a further step toward arriving at his or her taxable income. Therefore, above-the-line deductions are commonly known as *deductions FOR adjusted gross income*, whereas below-the-line deductions are commonly known as *deductions FROM adjusted gross income*.

While there are many ramifications regarding whether a deduction is above or below the line, a particular group of taxpayers become more susceptible to audits based on how these deductions are taken. Deductions for adjusted gross income consist of two categories. The first is business expenses that a taxpayer incurred in earning his or her gross income. The second category is comprised of a handful of specific expenditures that various sections of the I.R.C. have labeled as deductions for adjusted gross income, but these do not generally have the same audit potential as business expenses. Both categories of deductions for adjusted gross income will reduce the amount of an eligible taxpayer's income that is eventually subject to income taxation by the amount of the deduction. However, the deductions for adjusted gross income consisting of business expenses also reduce the amount of a taxpayer's gross income that is subject to self-employment tax, whereas the specific deductions from adjusted gross income that are created by various sections of the I.R.C. do not affect the amount of a taxpayer's gross income that is subject to self-employment tax.

Since most self-employed taxpayers in the U.S. currently pay more in self-employment taxes than they do in federal income taxes, they are generally especially eager to maximize the business deductions that will reduce both self-employment taxes and income taxes. As a result, some self-employed taxpayers yield to the temptation to overstate their business expenses, often by taking a deduction for expenses that simply do not qualify for deduction as business expenses. Employees who work for wages or salaries are not entitled to take business deductions, and this lack of opportunity to evade taxes by inflating business deductions is why employees are much less likely to be chosen for audit by the IRS than are self-employed taxpayers.

AUDIT ALERT

Self-employed taxpayers often overstate their business expenses by taking a deduction for expenses that simply do not qualify, resulting in an increased audit potential.

Qualifying to Take Business Deductions

Whether or not a given expenditure qualifies as a business deduction for adjusted gross income is determined by I.R.C. §162. Section 162 permits such deduction for "ordinary and necessary expenses paid or incurred during the taxable year in carrying on a trade or business." As is often the case with relatively broad provisions, application of I.R.C. §162 can prove troublesome, and is often the source of conflict between taxpayers and the IRS. Auditors not only require substantiation that deducted business expenditures were actually incurred, but also that they were ordinary and necessary.

The first step in taking a business deduction is to prove that you actually had a business. Internal Revenue Code §162 requires that a taxpayer incur expenses in the course of carrying on a trade or business in order to be allowed to deduct all of the expenses incurred in association with the activity. Obviously, there are situations when whether you were operating a trade or business is clear. However, most cases in which there is a question as to whether a person is actually engaged in a trade or business arise when the participant is involved only part-time or sporadically. Your side business or that extra work you do on weekends or for fun can cause real problems.

In order to be considered to be carrying on a trade or business, a self-employed taxpayer must have begun the endeavor with the intent to make a profit, must consistently and significantly participate in the venture, must demonstrate a commitment to the enterprise, and must conduct the operation in a businesslike manner. This sounds easy, but it knocks out the for-fun, hobby business that you are trying to claim expenses against. Activities engaged in that are not designed to make a profit, no matter how expensive, will not be considered a business or trade, but instead will be classified as a hobby by the IRS. Taking expenses for a hobby activity will make you vulnerable for an audit. Luckily, the fact that your business activity (as opposed to your hobby activities) actually generates a loss (rather than a profit) will not

AUDIT ALERT

Taking expenses for a hobby activity will make you vulnerable for an audit.

be fatal to it being considered a trade or business, as long as it was started with the intent to make a profit.

You can help prove that your activity is in fact a business by showing your commitment to it. Commitment to an enterprise may be demonstrated by such things as attendance at seminars or trade shows, taking formal courses to gain expertise in operating the business, or engaging in any other activity aimed at improving your ability to operate the enterprise profitably.

As indicated, if a purported business activity is determined not to be a trade or business, it will likely be classified as a hobby, and the allowable deduction for expenses will be limited to the amount necessary to offset gross income from the activity, thereby eliminating the deductibility of any losses generated by the venture. Moreover, even if you make a profit from your hobby and are allowed to take a deduction for the expenses associated with it, those expenses will have to be taken on Schedule A of Form 1040, and as you will learn in the subsequent section on itemized deductions, such deductions may not reduce your tax liability at all. Therefore, if you intend to engage in a part-time business that is likely to initially generate losses, you would be well advised to participate in those types of activities that support your contention that the part-time activity is a business. This will allow you to use the losses to offset income from your primary occupation and overcome losing the offset in the event of an audit.

Audit Alert

If you intend to engage in a part-time business that is likely to initially generate losses, you should also participate in activities that support the contention that the part-time activity is a business and not just a hobby.

The Ordinary and Necessary Requirement

In the event that the IRS challenges the validity of a business expense deduction, you will have the burden of proving that those expenses are *ordinary and necessary*. Several allowable business expenses are enumerated in

I.R.C. §162, making the ordinary and necessary determination for the self-employed taxpayer easy. Included are salary expenses, travel expenses, and rent. However, they are just a starting point, and any other business-related expenses may be deducted as long as they are shown to be both ordinary and necessary.

There is no clear-cut test to determine whether or not an expense is ordinary for the party wishing to deduct it. There have been numerous court cases over whether or not an expense was ordinary. In general, the courts have traditionally considered the issues of whether a business expense should be considered ordinary for a given taxpayer from two distinctly separate points of view. On the one hand, courts consider whether a given expense that a party deducted was appropriate in light of the type of activity involved. This does not necessarily look to whether the expenditures are of the type typically incurred by other taxpayers in their field or even that they were historically incurred by the party in question. The key determinant seems to be whether the expenditure was a reasonable one for that taxpayer at the time it was made. As long as there was a reasonable business purpose for the expenditure, it will likely be regarded as reasonable, and therefore ordinary, even if it does not result in any improvement in the profitability of the business activity. If you have an expense that may not be commonly associated with your trade or business, document at the time of the expense why you are making the purchase and what you intend to do with it. This will not automatically make it an ordinary expense, but it will help prove that you had a reasonable and rational reason for making it.

Another aspect of ordinary that courts analyze in considering whether or not a business expense should be deductible focuses on the reasonableness of

AUDIT ALERT

If you have an expense that may not be commonly associated with your trade or business, document at the time of the expense why you are making the purchase and what you intend to do with it.

the *amount* of the expenditure. Expenditures for business purposes that are clearly ordinary will likely still be considered nondeductible if they are considered *extravagant*. The determination as to whether a business expenditure is reasonable or lavish must be made on an individual basis, depending on the circumstances of the expenditure and the nature of the taxpayer's business.

The concept of necessary as it is used in determining whether a business expenditure qualifies as a deductible business expense has also been the topic of analysis in numerous court cases. It is clear that the word *necessary* as it is used in I.R.C. §162 to describe deductible business expense is not to be construed as essential or indispensable. In practice, the requirement that an expense must be necessary in order to be deductible is not much different than the requirement that it must be ordinary. As long as it can be shown that the expenditure was reasonable, both from the perspective that it would be beneficial to the self-employed taxpayer in conducting his or her business and that it was not lavish, it should qualify as a necessary expenditure for tax purposes.

Nonbusiness Adjustments for Adjusted Gross Income

There are a number of specific deductions for adjusted gross income that are set forth in individual statutes. Some of these deductions are available only to self-employed taxpayers, even though they do not have to show that they were ordinary and necessary business expenses, and others are available to taxpayers in general, as long as they meet the requirements to qualify for the deductions.

Deductions Available Only to the Self-Employed

Taxpayers are allowed to take a deduction for adjusted gross income for one-half of the self-employment taxes that they pay.

Since only workers with self-employment income will pay self-employment taxes, the deduction will obviously be limited to taxpayers who are self-employed to at least some extent. The deduction is based on a very elementary mathematical calculation that merely involves determining 50% of the amount of self-employment taxes that are shown on a taxpayer's tax return. Therefore, disputes seldom arise between taxpayers and the IRS over this deduction.

Self-employed individuals are allowed to take a deduction for adjusted gross income for the premiums that they pay for health insurance. In order to be eligible for this deduction, taxpayers cannot take a deduction for health insurance that exceeds their earnings from self-employment, and must not be eligible for subsidized coverage from an employer of theirs or their spouse's. Congress is considering eliminating this deduction and making health insurance premiums that are paid by employers taxable, as well, in order to reduce budget deficits.

Payments by self-employed taxpayers into any of a variety of retirement arrangements, such as Individual Retirement Arrangements (IRAs), Simplified Employee Plans (SEPs), Savings Incentive Match Plan for Employees (Simple IRA), profit-sharing plans, and 401(k) plans, can be used as deductions for adjusted gross income. For the most part, these plans merely postpone taxation until such time as the contributions to the plan and the earnings generated by them are paid out to the participant. Each plan has its own maximum limits and formula for calculating those limits for

DEDUCTIONS AVAILABLE ONLY TO THE SELF-EMPLOYED

- Self-employment taxes
- Premiums paid for health insurance
- Payments into some retirement arrangements, such as some Individual Retirement Arrangements (IRAs), Simplified Employee Plans (SEPs), Savings Incentive Match Plan for Employees (Simple IRA), profit-sharing plans, and 401(k) plans

making deductible contributions. Some of the retirement arrangements are also available to taxpayers who are not considered to be self-employed, such as employees whose employers do not have retirement plans.

Contributions to plans that discriminate by making larger percentages of contributions for more highly compensated employees are generally ineligible for the deduction. Auditors closely scrutinize such plans for that type of discrimination during audits of self-employed taxpayers who have deducted contributions to retirement plans. Therefore, it is advisable to consult with a professional who is well versed in the rules governing the deductibility of contributions to such plans, in order to ensure that any deductions taken will be validated by an IRS audit. In many instances professional advice is available without charge from parties who market various retirement plans.

Deductions for Adjusted Gross Income that are Available in General

Some of the deductions for adjusted gross income that are available to taxpayers regardless of whether or not they are self-employed—such as the deductions for qualified educator expense, penalty for early withdrawal of savings, interest on student loans, and alimony paid—are the result of such straight-forward requirements and limits that there is little room for misunderstanding. Typically, disputes over their deductibility are rare, with the exception being when the IRS finds itself in the middle of a dispute between parties as to whether payments constitute alimony for tax purposes.

DEDUCTIONS FOR ADJUSTED GROSS INCOME THAT ARE AVAILABLE IN GENERAL
- Qualified educator expense
- Penalty for early withdrawal of savings
- Interest on student loans
- Alimony paid
- Moving expenses
- Tuition and fees

The deduction for moving expenses, which is also available as a deduction for adjusted gross income for taxpayers in general, is subject to some relatively complex rules. In order to qualify for the deduction, a taxpayer must move a certain distance in order to obtain or retain employment, and then must work at the new location for a certain minimum time. The rules for determining what constitutes a qualified distance, as well as the time test for the new employment, are what make calculating the deduction difficult. Furthermore, not all of the expenditures related to relocation qualify for the moving expense deduction. Since moving expense deductions are often sizable, and mistakes in applying the complex rules for the deduction are common, such deductions may raise the likelihood of an audit. Taxpayers with moving expenses would probably be wise to engage the services of a professional tax return preparer for that year.

Still another deduction for adjusted gross income that is available to taxpayers in general is the deduction for tuition and fees. There are several provisions available to taxpayers that permit some form of deduction for tuition and fees, including some tax credits. Each of the provisions has its own requirements and limitations, and taxpayers cannot generally avail themselves of more than one of the write-offs. Once again, due to the complexity of the provisions regarding tax deductions and credits for tuition and fees, it may be best to engage the services of a professional tax return preparer to evaluate the appropriateness of such write-offs. You do not want to find out in audit that the write-offs you have been taking, possibly for several years, are all disallowed, placing you in a situation in which you face a significant tax deficiency along with penalties and interest.

AUDIT ALERT

Since moving expense deductions are often sizable, and mistakes in applying the complex rules for the deduction are common, such deductions may raise the likelihood of an audit.

Deductions from Adjusted Gross Income

Once a taxpayer has subtracted his or her deductions for adjusted gross income in order to arrive at adjusted gross income, the only remaining allowable deductions are the deductions *from* adjusted gross income. These deductions are, for the most part, unaffected by whether a taxpayer's income was earned from self-employment activity, work as an employee, or some other source. The allowable deductions from adjusted gross income take the form of either a standard deduction or the total of certain itemized deductions.

Itemized Deductions

Itemized deductions seem like a good way to lower your income, and thus, your tax burden. While they certainly can do that, compared to business deductions and deductions for adjusted gross income, taxpayers generally find that itemized deductions are not as beneficial as they may first appear.

Itemized deductions are subject to a number of limitations. While the deductions previously discussed may also be subject to certain limitations, most taxpayers will find those deductions to be almost dollar-for-dollar of expense versus deduction—if you spent $100, you can deduct $100. For many of the categories for itemized deductions, you will not qualify until you have spent beyond a certain amount, and then it will only be the amount beyond that threshold that is deductible.

Plus, most taxpayers are allowed to take a relatively sizable standard deduction in lieu of itemizing deductions, which causes itemized deductions to be of absolutely no value to them until they exceed the amount of their standard deduction. Even taxpayers whose itemized deductions exceed their allowable standard deductions will realize tax savings only to the extent of the excess itemized deductions. Therefore, taxpayers who are motivated to incur expenditures because they are tax deductible may simply be bringing the amount of their itemized deductions closer to their standard deductions, or just barely over their standard deductions, and will realize little or no tax benefit from the expenditures. It is important to remember that deductions reduce your income subject to taxation. If you are in the 25% tax bracket, you then save roughly 25¢ on your taxes for every $1 spent on a deductible expenditure. If you are not careful, you can find yourself in a situation in which you are actually losing 75¢ for every $1 you are spending to increase your itemized deductions.

Congress has traditionally allowed most taxpayers to take a federal tax deduction for several categories of expenditures. There is no real pattern or basis to explain why some expenditures may be deducted while others may not, or why some of the deductions are subject to limitations and others are not. Generally, taxpayers must meet rather specific requirements in order to qualify for an itemized deduction, and there will be little or no room for argument if those requirements are not met. The various categories of itemized deductions follow.

Medical and Dental Expenses
Internal Revenue Code Section 213 permits taxpayers to take a deduction for medical and dental expenses. Included among the deductible medical and dental expenses are payments made for both prevention and treatment or cure of disease, including the cost of prescription drugs, prescribed long-term care for the chronically ill, and the cost of transportation to receive medical care. For many taxpayers, the largest component of the medical and dental expenses that they may deduct is the health insurance premiums that they pay. However, in order to be deductible, the premiums must actually be paid by the taxpayer rather than by his or her employer. This approach is justified by the fact that taxpayers are not taxed on the health insurance premiums paid by their employers on their behalves. The deductibility of health insurance premiums that are actually paid by taxpayers and the exclusion from taxable income of any such premiums paid by employers for their employees come with a cost to taxpayers in the form of losing the

right to take a deduction for any medical expenses that are paid for them by their health insurance companies.

Even though health insurance premiums and the uninsured portion of health care expenses may add up to a sizable sum, very few taxpayers actually benefit from this deduction due to significant limitations having been placed on the deductibility of these expenses. First, taxpayers are required to reduce the total of their qualified out-of-pocket medical and dental expenses, including the health insurance premiums that they paid, by an amount equal to 7.5% of their adjusted gross income. This step in the calculations generally leaves only those taxpayers who had extremely high uninsured medical and dental expenses and health insurance premiums with anything to deduct. Additionally, unless the total of a taxpayer's itemized deductions that appear on Schedule A of Form 1040, which is where the medical and dental expense deduction is taken, exceed his or her standard deduction, he or she will receive no benefit from the deduction.

Self-employed taxpayers who are not covered by a subsidized health care plan provided by an employer or a spouse's employer may elect to take a deduction for their health care insurance premiums as a deduction for adjusted gross income. The deduction, which is taken on the front of Form 1040, provides those who are eligible to take it with a tremendous advantage since the deduction is not subject to being reduced by any percentage of the taxpayer's adjusted gross income. Furthermore, the deduction may be taken regardless of whether the taxpayer itemizes his or her other deductions on Schedule A of Form 1040. However, if a deduction for adjusted gross income is taken for health insurance premiums, a taxpayer

AUDIT ALERT

Audits over the amount of a taxpayer's deduction for taxes paid are rare, although verification of deductions for taxes paid may be included in a general audit.

cannot also take an itemized deduction for the same premiums on Schedule A of Form 1040.

Taxpayers who own 2% or more of a small business also qualify to take their health care premiums as a deduction for adjusted gross income if they otherwise meet the requirements to qualify for the deduction. However, taxpayers who are not owners but are mere employees of companies do not qualify for the option of taking a deduction for adjusted gross income for the health insurance premiums that they pay even if their employers do not provide a subsidized health care program. Their only option will be to use the health care premiums that they pay, in calculating their itemized deductions on Schedule A of Form 1040 and then determining whether they are better off taking those deductions or their allowable standard deduction.

Taxes Paid

Among the various taxes that individuals pay, some—such as state, local, and foreign income taxes, and state, local, and foreign property taxes—qualify as itemized deductions under I.R.C. §164. Still other taxes that individuals commonly pay do not qualify as itemized deductions. Among them are federal income taxes, FICA taxes, estate and gift taxes, and any payments to governmental entities for which goods, services, or personal privileges are received.

Proof of tax payments is generally readily available. For most, your W-2 will contain the amount of state income tax you can deduct, and your bank, mortgage holder or county assessor's office will provide you with what you paid in property taxes. Since the IRS also receives this information, there is no real room for argument over the deductibility of the various types of taxes that are levied. Audits over the amount of a taxpayer's deduction for taxes paid are rare, although verification of deductions for taxes paid may well be included in a general audit of a taxpayer.

Congress has reinstated the provisions that allow taxpayers to choose to deduct their state and local general sales taxes *instead* of their state and local income taxes. They are not allowed to deduct both. Taxpayers who reside in states that do not have a state or local income tax will obviously choose to take the sales tax deduction, but those in states with both types of taxes will have to calculate each of the two and determine which one is the larger. Taxpayers are permitted to calculate their sales taxes using their sales receipts that contain their actual sales tax payments or they may simply use tables provided by the IRS.

Itemized Interest Expenses

Although at one time U.S. tax law permitted taxpayers to deduct any interest expenses that they incurred as an itemized deduction, current law limits the itemized deduction available to individuals for interest expenses to home mortgage interest and investment interest. However, even those taxpayers who have incurred interest expenses that qualify for the itemized deduction must meet certain requirements, or the right to take the deduction will be lost.

The Home Mortgage Interest Deduction. For purposes of establishing that interest paid constitutes home mortgage interest that is deductible under I.R.C. §163, it must be shown that the loan on which the interest was paid was obtained to buy a main home or second home, or the loan must have been a second mortgage, line of credit, or home equity loan on a main or second home. Additionally, the taxpayer must be legally liable on a valid, bona fide debt that is secured by a legitimate mortgage on a qualified home, and the mortgage must be evidenced by a binding promissory note and collateralized with the property being mortgaged. Although the specific methods of collateralizing loans on real property differ somewhat from state to state, they all share the common denominator of a written grant, such as a mortgage or deed of trust, that is signed by the owners of the property, and that authorizes a designated party to foreclose on the loan if the debtor fails to make timely payments, and that is generally recorded at the same place where deeds are recorded.

Taxpayers who do not have home mortgage interest to deduct rarely find it advantageous to itemize deductions, and simply take the standard deduction. Therefore, due to the impact of the home mortgage interest deduction, financial institutions who collect such interest are required to report the amount of interest that they receive from each taxpayer on a Form 1099, a copy of which must be sent to both the IRS and the taxpayer. This provides the IRS with information with which to verify the validity of a taxpayer's home mortgage interest deduction. Interest received on mortgage loans from entities that are not financial institutions must be reported on the recipient's tax return, along with the name and Social Security number of the debtor, so that the payments can be verified, since such recipients are not required to send out 1099 forms.

If a taxpayer's interest deduction exceeds the amount of interest reported to the IRS by all of the recipients, the IRS will likely contact the taxpayer for an explanation, if not for a full audit. Disputes also can arise between taxpayers and the IRS over the deductibility of certain expenses associated with obtaining a mortgage, since some of those expenses—such as discount points and origination fees—may qualify as deductible mortgage interest, whereas others—such as appraisal fees and the cost to record deeds and mortgages—are definitely not deductible as a form of mortgage interest expense. Also, if the total indebtedness exceeds the fair market value of the property mortgaged, the interest deduction must be reduced to the level that would be paid if the total indebtedness equaled the fair market value of the property mortgaged.

Investment Interest. Section 163(d)(5) of the I.R.C. allows taxpayers to deduct interest that they pay on indebtedness

AUDIT ALERT

If a taxpayer's interest deduction exceeds the amount of interest reported to the IRS by all of the recipients, the IRS will likely contact the taxpayer for an explanation, if not for a full audit.

incurred to acquire investments, which I.R.C. §469(e)(1) defines as items that generate income from "interest, dividends, annuities or royalties not derived in the course of a trade or business." No interest deduction is permitted on investments that generate tax-exempt income, passive activities (those in which a taxpayer did not materially participate), or interest incurred on *straddles* (taking a simultaneous long and short position in the same security). Also, no deduction for investment interest will be allowed to the extent that the investment interest exceeds the taxpayer's net investment income.

Charitable Contributions

Under the provisions of I.R.C. §170, cash contributions and the fair market value of contributions of property made to qualified organizations up to an amount equal to 50% of the individual *donor's* adjusted gross income for the year are generally deductible by the donor as charitable gifts on Schedule A. This is only allowed provided that the contributions were made to what are known as *50% limit organizations*, which include most charitable organizations. The charitable organization to which a donation is made should be able to inform donors whether or not it is a 50% limit organization.

No deduction may be taken for a contribution to the extent that the donor received benefits in exchange. However, if the donor receives benefits with a smaller fair market value than the amount of the contribution, a deduction may still be taken for the difference.

For example, if you were to buy a ticket to a charitable dinner that cost $100 per ticket, but the meal had a fair market value of $30, you would be able to deduct $70.

A sale of property to a qualified organization at less than fair market value, known as a *bargain sale*, will result in a

AUDIT ALERT

Taxpayers who take a charitable contribution deduction arising from a bargain sale to a charitable organization should anticipate a challenge from the IRS when the deduction is sizable.

deductible contribution to the extent that the fair market value of the property that was sold exceeds its sale price. For example, if you sell your $1,000 baseball card for $100 to a qualified charity, you can deduct the $900 as a charitable contribution. Donors of property that has appreciated in value are allowed to take a deduction for the full appreciated value if the appreciation consists of long-term capital gain, which is gain from the sale of certain property held for over one year. Taxpayers who take a charitable contribution deduction arising from a bargain sale to a charitable organization should anticipate a challenge from the IRS when the deduction is sizable. This is due to the fact that the size of the deduction is determined by the fair market value that was attributed to the property that was sold, and fair market value, in such cases, is a matter of opinion, since the taxpayer's contention is that the sale price is not the property's fair market value, but rather, an amount less than fair market value. In order to withstand the challenge of an IRS audit concerning the value of a contribution arising from a bargain sale, it is imperative that the taxpayer get an appraisal from a certified appraiser at the time of the sale. Even then, the IRS may counter with an appraisal of its own and challenge the taxpayer's deduction when their appraisal is significantly below the taxpayer's appraisal.

No deduction is allowed for gifts made to individuals or to non-qualified organizations. In order to prevent donors from being able to give gifts to qualified organizations so they can take a tax deduction for them, and then having that organization give the gift to the unqualified party that the donor wishes to benefit, donors are prohibited from taking a deduction for donations when they stipulate that the benefit of their gift is to go to a specific non-qualified recipient. However, donors can make gifts to qualified organizations and specify that they are to be used for some particular purpose, such as providing relief to victims of a certain hurricane, and they will still be permitted to take a deduction for their contributions.

No deduction is available for the contribution of one's time or service, even when the contribution is made to a qualified organization. However, out-of-pocket expenses—such as the cost of transportation or the cost of buying and cleaning uniforms—associated with contributed services are deductible. However, the cost of child care necessary to permit a person to perform volunteer work is not an expense that is deductible as a charitable contribution.

Taxpayers must maintain adequate records to substantiate their charitable contributions, and as the amount of the contribution goes up, the recordkeeping requirement becomes more stringent. Cash contributions, which include donations by check, credit card, and payroll deduction, as well as currency, of less than $250 can be substantiated by a cancelled check, an account statement from the recipient showing the amount and date of the contribution, or the taxpayer's own written records showing the name of the recipient and the amount and date of the contribution. These records should be kept as contributions are made (the IRS does not want you going back and recreating records, so it requires that you make a record of the contribution at the time you make it). As long as no single contribution to a charity exceeds $250, it will qualify as a gift of less than $250, even if other contributions to the same charity would put the combined total of those contributions well over $250.

Deductions for cash contributions, other than by payroll deduction, in excess of $250 each must be supported by a written acknowledgment from the qualified organization receiving them, stating the amount of the contributions and the value of goods or services, if any, that were received as a result of the contributions. This acknowledgment must be received by the taxpayer on or before the earlier of the date the taxpayer files a return for the year in which the contribution was made or the due date for such return, including extensions.

Noncash contributions require the most stringent documentation to support a charitable contribution deduction. There are four different categories of noncash contributions. Each has separate requirements for supporting a deduction. The categories are determined by the fair market value of each contribution.

Documentation of noncash contributions of less than $250 requires a receipt from the recipient showing its name and location, the date of the gift, and a reasonably detailed description of the property that is donated. Taxpayers are not required to combine separate noncash gifts made to a given donee over the course of the taxable year in determining the value of a noncash gift. Also, the donor must maintain additional records for each donated item, reflecting the name and address of the donee, the date of the gift, a reasonably detailed description of the property, the value of the contribution and how it was determined, and any terms or conditions attached to the gift.

A taxpayer who takes a charitable gift deduction for noncash donations of items valued at $250 to $500 must obtain and keep a written acknowledgment of the contribution from the recipient. An acknowledgment for each such gift is required, although a single acknowledgment can be used to show multiple contributions. The acknowledgment must show the name and address of the donee, the date of the gift, a reasonably detailed description of the property, and whether goods or services were given to the donor as a result of the contribution, and if so, the estimated fair market value of them. The charitable organization is not required to estimate the value of the donated property. The donor must obtain the acknowledgment on or before the earlier of the date he or she files his or her tax return for the year of the contribution or the due date for filing the return, including any extensions. The taxpayer must also maintain additional records with the same information as what is contained in such records for noncash gifts valued at less than $250.

Deductions for donations of noncash property valued at more than $500 but not over $5,000 must be supported by an acknowledgment from the recipient that meets the

AUDIT ALERT

Due to the potential for abuse, deductions for large amounts of noncash contributions are likely to trigger an IRS audit.

requirements for such acknowledgments for gifts valued at between $250 and $500. Taxpayers are also required to maintain their own records for noncash gifts that contain the same information as such records for smaller noncash gifts, plus information as to how and when the donor got the property and the donor's cost or other basis in the donated property.

Those who take deductions for noncash property valued in excess of $5,000 must meet all of the requirements for supporting a deduction for noncash contributions valued at over $500 but not over $5,000, plus they must obtain a qualified written appraisal of the donated property. For purposes of determining whether the value of noncash donations exceeds $5,000, taxpayers must combine all similar items donated to all donees during the taxable year. The appraisal requirement does not apply to donations of publicly traded securities.

Most taxpayers are permitted to take their charitable contributions on Schedule A of Form 1040. However, taxpayers who take deductions for total noncash contributions of over $500 must also file Form 8283, which calls for extensive information concerning donated property, acknowledgment by the donee, and requires attachment of appraisals when they are necessary. Due to the potential for abuse, deductions for large amounts of noncash contributions are likely to trigger an IRS audit and failure to fully substantiate the value of those contributions to the satisfaction of the auditor will likely result in disallowance of some or all of the deduction.

Casualty and Theft Losses

Individuals are not allowed to take a tax deduction for ordinary wear and tear that diminishes the value of their personal property. However, when a taxpayer's personal property is damaged or destroyed by an identifiable event that is sudden, unexpected, and unusual—such as fire, storm, vandalism, or auto accident—I.R.C. §165 allows a limited itemized deduction for the loss. Such a deduction is also allowed for losses due to theft— such as burglary, robbery, shoplifting, and even blackmail, extortion, or kidnapping for ransom—but not for property that was merely misplaced. For this deduction to be of any benefit, the monetary loss generally has to be extremely significant.

The amount of a party's casualty or theft loss is determined by subtracting the post-loss fair market value of items subject to a casualty or theft loss from the taxpayer's adjusted basis in the items, and then further reducing the loss by any insurance or other reimbursement received or expected. The post-loss fair market value of unrecovered stolen property and property totally destroyed by casualty will be zero after the loss, and therefore, the decline in the value of such property due to the loss will be equal to its fair market value. In determining the fair market value of property involved in a casualty or theft loss, no allowance can be included for the fact that replacement cost may exceed the property's fair market value, the property may hold sentimental value for the taxpayer, or the taxpayer incurred costs incidental to the loss (such as the need to temporarily obtain a rental car or the necessity to get medical treatment for injuries associated with the loss).

Calculating the Personal Deduction for Casualty and Theft Losses. Once a determination has been made as to the amount of a taxpayer's casualty or theft loss, two separate limits must then be applied in order to determine the amount of the loss that the party will be allowed to take as a personal deduction. First, the total loss from each casualty or theft event must be reduced by $100. Then, the total losses from all casualties and thefts, less the $100 deduction per event, are added together for the taxable year, and an amount equal to

AUDIT ALERT

Claiming a deduction for a casualty or theft loss will almost certainly increase a taxpayer's chances of being audited.

10% of the taxpayer's adjusted gross income for the year must be subtracted from that total. The remaining balance is the amount that the taxpayer is eligible to deduct as a casualty or theft loss on his or her personal tax return. In light of the limitations placed on the casualty and theft loss deductions, they are sufficiently rare that the IRS can devote time to take a look at practically all of them. Furthermore, since valuation issues with the potential for abuse through overstating values of damaged or stolen property are often involved, claiming a deduction for a casualty or theft loss will almost certainly increase a taxpayer's chances of being audited.

EXAMPLE:

In June, you were involved in an auto accident that totally destroyed your personal car and your antique pocket watch. You had bought the car for $30,000. The fair market value (FMV) of the car just before the accident was $17,500. Its FMV just after the accident was $180 (scrap value). Your insurance company reimbursed you $16,000.

Your watch was not insured. You had purchased it for $250. Its FMV just before the accident was $500. Your adjusted gross income for the year the accident occurred is $97,000. Your casualty loss deduction is zero, figured as follows.

		Car	Watch
1.	Adjusted basis (cost)	$30,000	$250
2.	FMV before accident	$17,500	$500
3.	FMV after accident	180	-0-
4.	Decrease in FMV (line 2 - line 3)	$17,320	$500

5.	Loss		
	(smaller of line 1 or line 4)	$17,320	$250
6.	Subtract insurance	$16,000	-0-
7.	Loss after reimbursement	$1,320	$250
8.	Total loss		$1,570
9.	Subtract		$100
10.	Loss after $100 rule		$1,470
11.	Subtract 10% of $97,000 AGI		$9,700
12.	Casualty loss deduction		-0-

Miscellaneous Deductions

The final two categories of itemized deductions on Schedule A of Form 1040 are both less specific than the other categories of itemized deductions. The category shown on Schedule A as "Job Expenses and Most Other Miscellaneous Deductions" provides for the deduction of unreimbursed business expenses incurred by employees in the performance of their jobs. Included among those deductible expenses are travel expenses, job-related educational expenses, and the cost of their samples and supplies. Self-employed individuals should never take a deduction for expenses that are related to their self-employment activities as a job expense on Schedule A. Self-employed taxpayers are allowed to take their job-related expenses as business deductions on Schedule C, which will, unquestionably, be more beneficial than an itemized deduction, since business deductions reduce the amount of a party's income that is subject to self-employment taxes.

All of the deductions taken under the "Job Expenses and Most Other Miscellaneous

AUDIT ALERT

Taxpayers who take sizable deductions for job-related expenses are more likely to be audited than those who do not.

Deductions" category must be reduced by an amount equal to 2% of the adjusted gross income of the taxpayer taking the deduction, which will significantly reduce, if not altogether eliminate, such deductions. However, a significant number of taxpayers still take sizable deductions for job-related expense, and since such deductions lend themselves to being overstated due to fabricating expenditures or including ineligible expenditures, taxpayers who take such deductions are more likely to be audited than those who do not. Therefore, taxpayers with job-related expenses need to meticulously maintain records of those expenditures.

The final category of itemized deductions on Schedule A is "Other Miscellaneous Deductions." The miscellaneous deductions in this category differ from those in the category that includes job expenses in that their total is not reduced by an amount equal to 2% of the taxpayer's adjusted gross income. There are very few items that qualify for this type of deduction. They are specifically listed in the Schedule A instructions. Among the more common ones are casualty and theft losses from income-producing property; gambling losses up to the amount of the taxpayer's reported gambling winnings; expenses incurred by a disabled person that are related to work and necessitated by the party's disability; and, federal estate tax paid on inheritances consisting of wages that the deceased had earned but not received, and that were included in the heirs' earnings for income tax purposes, known as *income in respect of a decedent.*

The General Limitations on Itemized Deductions

As previously discussed, after reducing qualified medical and dental expenses by 7.5% of their adjusted gross incomes, reducing casualty losses by 10% of their adjusted gross incomes, and reducing job-related and most other miscellaneous deductions by 2% of their adjusted gross incomes, only those taxpayers whose total itemized deductions exceed their allowable standard deductions will benefit from itemizing deductions, and even those taxpayers will benefit only to the extent that their itemized deductions exceed their allowable standard deductions. However, having itemized deductions that exceed the applicable standard deduction will not guarantee that a taxpayer will benefit from itemizing deductions. This is due to the provisions of I.R.C. §68, which requires taxpayers with relatively high incomes to reduce their itemized deductions. As your income increases, the amount of the itemized deductions you can take decreases. There is a worksheet in the instructions to Schedule A for calculating the reductions in itemized deductions that are required of those with high incomes.

The Standard Deduction

In lieu of itemizing deductions on Schedule A of Form 1040, I.R.C. §63 permits taxpayers to take a standard deduction, and in some instances, an additional standard deduction. A standard base amount is provided for in Section 63, which further provides that the standard deduction base is to be adjusted to reflect increases in the cost of living, but rounded down to the nearest $50 increment. A certain percentage of the base amount of the standard deduction is then taken to establish the standard deduction for each taxpayer based on the party's filing status. The standard deduction is now over $5,000 for individual filers, with higher amounts for the other filing statuses.

Determining Filing Status

Marital status is the primary determinant of a taxpayer's filing status. Among the categories of filing status are *single, married filing jointly*, and *married filing separately*. A taxpayer's marital status on the last day of the tax year will determine the party's filing status. In the event of the death of a spouse, the survivor is still permitted to use the status of married filing jointly for the year in which the party's spouse died. For the two years following the year in which a party's spouse died, the surviving spouse may be eligible to file as a *qualifying widow(er) with dependent child*. In order to qualify for this status, the surviving spouse must have been eligible to file a joint return with the deceased spouse for the year in which that spouse died, must not have remarried by the end of the year for which the status is chosen, and must have paid more than half the cost of maintaining the primary home for the year in which the taxpayer and at least one child that the taxpayer can claim as a dependent resided. Those who qualify for this status are entitled to use the married filing jointly tax rates and the highest standard deduction as an alternative to itemizing deductions.

There is another category of filing status known as *head of household*, which is available to unmarried people who provided over half the cost of maintaining a home for someone that lived with them and that they can claim as a dependent. A married person who lived apart from his or her spouse for the last six months of the year; who pays more than half of the cost of keeping up his or her home, which was also the main home of a child, stepchild, or adopted child for over half the tax year; and who is eligible to claim an exemption for that child, or would have been eligible to claim such an exemption except for the fact that the noncustodial parent is allowed to claim the exemption, will also qualify for head of household filing status. The standard deduction for those who qualify for head of household status, although not as large as the standard deduction for those filing married filing jointly, is substantially larger than the amount allowed for those filing as single, and the tax rates are also generally significantly lower than the rates for taxpayers filing as single.

Additional Standard Deduction Allowance for the Aged or Blind

An additional standard deduction allowance is provided for those who are 65 years of age or older and for those who are blind or partially blind. For purposes of this added allowance, a person is considered to be *partially blind* if his or her vision cannot be corrected to better than 20/200 or his or her field of vision is 20 degrees or less. If a party is both blind or partially blind and 65 years of age or older, he or she is entitled to two additional standard deduction allowances.

The Standard Deduction for Those Claimed as a Dependent by Others

A taxpayer who can be claimed as a dependent by another taxpayer may be limited to a greatly reduced standard deduction. Such parties have, in recent years, been limited to a standard deduction that is the larger of a small base amount that is somewhat less than $1,000, or an amount equal to their earned income plus $250, but not to exceed the standard deduction for their filing status.

Those Ineligible for the Standard Deduction

There are three groups of taxpayers who are ineligible to take the standard deduction. In each case, the party's standard deduction is deemed to be zero. A married taxpayer who files as married filing separately and whose spouse itemizes deductions must itemize deductions as well. This requirement prevents married couples from allocating all of their itemized deductions to one of the spouses and claiming a standard deduction for the other spouse.

Those who file tax returns for a tax year of less than twelve months due to their having changed their annual accounting period are ineligible to take a standard deduction. The standard deduction is supposed to reflect basic living costs for a year, and allowing such a deduction for a period of less than a year would result in an excessive allowance. There are no provisions in the U.S. Tax Code to permit a proration of the appropriate standard deduction in such cases.

Parties who are nonresident aliens or dual-status aliens during the year are not permitted to use the standard deduction for the year. A party who is both a resident alien for part of the year and a nonresident alien for the remainder is considered to be a dual-status alien.

Chapter Three
Exemptions

In calculating taxable income, a taxpayer is allowed to reduce adjusted gross income by not only the larger of the standard deduction or allowable itemized deductions, but also by any available allowance for exemptions. The exemptions that are available are personal exemptions and exemptions for dependents.

Personal Exemptions

Each taxpayer is allowed to take a personal exemption for him- or herself, unless he or she can be claimed as a dependent by some other taxpayer. Married taxpayers who file joint returns are allowed to take a personal exemption for each spouse. Even if a married taxpayer files a separate return, the party can still take a personal exemption for his or her spouse, as long as the spouse had no gross income and could not be claimed as a dependent by some other taxpayer, regardless of whether that party actually claimed the spouse. The fact that a party's spouse is a nonresident alien will not affect the right to take a personal exemption for the spouse, as long as the taxpayer is otherwise qualified to do so. If a spouse dies, the surviving spouse may still claim a personal exemption for the deceased spouse for the year of the spouse's death, provided that the surviving spouse did not remarry during that year. No personal exemption may be taken for a spouse if the couple is divorced or legally separated as of the last day of the year, even if the party seeking the exemption had fully supported the former spouse for the entire year in question.

Exemptions for Dependents

In addition to the personal exemption available to taxpayers and their spouses, exemptions may also be taken for dependents. However, they must meet the five dependency tests to qualify the taxpayer to take an exemption for them.

The Relationship Test

In order for a taxpayer to be entitled to take an exemption for someone as his or her dependent, that party must have either lived with him or her as a member of the party's household for the entire tax year or must be related to the taxpayer to the degree specified in I.R.C. §152. Those who are considered to be relatives of a taxpayer under the provisions of Section 152 are children, stepchildren, grandchildren, and great-grandchildren; brothers and sisters, including half brothers and sisters and stepbrothers and stepsisters; parents, stepparents, grandparents, and great-grandparents; aunts and uncles; nieces and nephews; parents and siblings of a spouse; and, sons-in-law and daughters-in-law. Any of the relationships created by marriage are not terminated by divorce or by the death of the taxpayer's blood relative.

The Citizenship or Residency Test

A person for whom a taxpayer wishes to take an exemption as a dependent must be a citizen or resident of the U.S., or a resident of Canada or Mexico. As long as the party meets this requirement for some part of the calendar year in which the taxpayer's tax year begins, the requirement of the test is considered met for the year.

The Joint Return Test

Generally, if a taxpayer is otherwise entitled to take an exemption for a dependent, but the dependent is married and files a joint return, the taxpayer will not be allowed to take the exemption. The lone exception to this provision is the situation in which a party's married dependent files a joint return with his or her spouse in order to claim a refund of taxes withheld from earnings, but would otherwise have such low earnings that no taxes would have been due for either of them if they had filed separate returns.

The Gross Income Test

In order to be entitled to take an exemption for a dependent, the dependent person cannot have gross income in excess of the amount of the exemption deduction. However, a parent is allowed to claim an exemption for his or her dependent child, regardless of how much the child earns, as long as that child is either under the age of 19 at the end of the year, or under the age of 24 at year's end and a full-time student for at least five calendar months during the calendar year. Even though parents may be allowed to take an exemption for dependent children with incomes of their own, the result will be that the children will not be allowed to take an exemption for themselves on their own returns.

The Support Test

To qualify to take an exemption deduction for a dependent, a taxpayer who is otherwise qualified to take the exemption must usually provide more than half of the support for that person. However, there are two exceptions to this rule.

Multiple Support Agreements

If two or more otherwise qualified people together provide over 50% of a party's support, but no individual person provides the party with over half of his or her total support, any otherwise qualified person who provides over 10% of the party's support may claim the exemption for the dependent, as long as every other qualified party who provided over 10% of the dependent's support signs a Form 2120, which is a *Multiple Support Declaration*, stating that they will not claim the exemption for the dependent. An executed Form 2120 from each otherwise qualified party who is not taking an exemption for someone that they provided over 10% of their support to must be included with the tax return of the taxpayer who does claim an exemption for the dependent. Taxpayers should keep a copy of each Form 2120 for their own records, as well.

Children of Divorced or Separated Parents

Normally, if a child's parents are divorced, legally separated under a written separation agreement, or they lived apart for the last six months of the calendar year, the parent who had custody of the child for the larger part of the year will be considered to have provided over half of the child's support and will be entitled to claim the child as a dependent for tax purposes. This rule will not apply if the noncustodial parent can show that he or she actually provided over half of the child's support for the year. If there is a divorce decree or a decree of separate maintenance that states which party will be entitled to claim an exemption for a couple's dependent child, the decree will govern.

AUDIT ALERT

There are a couple of situations in which exemptions can trigger an audit. The first is when more than one person claims the same person as a dependant for an exemption. The second occurs when the taxpayer is in a relatively high tax bracket and fails to make the required adjustment for the exemption deduction phaseout.

Audit Aspects of Tax Exemptions

There are a couple of situations in which exemptions can trigger an audit. The first is when more than one person claims the same person as a dependant for an exemption. In order to be allowed to take an exemption for a dependent, a taxpayer must supply the IRS with the claimed dependent's Social Security number and describe the relationship between the parties. The IRS automatically cross-references Social Security numbers to detect situations in which more than one taxpayer has claimed a person as their dependent. When this occurs, the IRS will contact the parties involved to make a determination as to whom, if anyone, is entitled to claim the exemption.

The second occurs when the taxpayer is in a relatively high tax bracket. Taxpayers with relatively large incomes must reduce their allowance for exemptions. Taxpayers whose incomes exceed a statutorily set threshold amount must reduce their exemptions deductions by 2% for every segment of $2,500 that their income exceeds the threshold amount, up to a maximum of 100%. The threshold amounts are adjusted for inflation each year and reflected in a worksheet, provided in the Form 1040 instructions, for calculating the exemption deduction phaseout. If a taxpayer fails to make the required adjustment, the IRS will recalculate the taxpayer's tax liability and notify him or her of the recalculation and resulting tax deficiency.

Chapter Four

Federal Income Taxes and Common Tax Credits

The method for calculating federal income tax liabilities is not appreciably different whether the taxpayers earned their incomes from working as someone else's employee, from self-employment activities, or as some form of investment or retirement fund. In fact, it is common for taxpayers to have income from a variety of sources during the course of a taxable year.

Regular Federal Income Taxes

Once the various sources of income and losses are transferred from the appropriate forms and schedules onto Form 1040, and all of the allowable deductions and exemptions are subtracted, the remaining balance, referred to as *taxable income*, is then subjected to the applicable rate of taxation to determine the taxpayer's federal income tax liability. The U.S. federal income tax is considered to be a *progressive tax* because the rates of taxation increase as taxpayers' taxable incomes increase. This progressiveness is accomplished in the U.S. by establishing income segments, known as *tax brackets*, and applying higher tax rates to higher segments of a taxpayer's income. As a taxpayer's income rises and enters higher tax brackets, the higher rates will apply only to the income in the higher bracket.

The lowest level of taxable income is taxed at 10%, followed by brackets of 15%, 25%, 28%, 33%, and 35% as taxable income rises. The amount of income that is taxed in each bracket depends on the taxpayer's filing status. Married taxpayers who file joint returns have the largest brackets at each level beneath the highest rate of taxation, which results in the lowest tax on a given amount of income for the various categories of taxpayers. Married taxpayers who file separately have the smallest amount of income that is taxed in each bracket below the maximum, resulting in the highest tax on a given amount of taxable income among the various categories of taxpayers. The size of the tax brackets for single taxpayers and heads of household fall between those for married taxpayers filing separately and married taxpayers filing jointly.

The instructions to Form 1040 contain a tax table that shows the tax liability for each filing status at various levels of annual ordinary income up to $100,000. Those who make in excess of $100,000 in ordinary income for the year must use the Tax Rate Schedules provided in the Form 1040 instructions to calculate their tax liability. Taxpayers who have some income in the form of long-term capital gains or dividends must calculate their tax liability using a worksheet found in the instructions to Schedule D of Form 1040 in order to prevent those gains from being taxed in excess of the maximum 15% tax rate that applies to most long-term capital gains and dividends.

AUDIT ALERT

The IRS's automated verification catches taxpayers who use the wrong tax table or otherwise miscalculate their tax liability.

It is not uncommon for taxpayers to use the wrong tax table or otherwise miscalculate their tax liability. When this occurs, it will generally come to light when the IRS submits the return to a routine automated verification. The result will usually be nothing more than a letter to the taxpayer explaining that it appears an error was made and requesting payment if the result is a tax deficiency or stating that a refund check will soon be forthcoming if the error resulted in overpayment.

Alternative Minimum Tax

Some taxpayers with relatively substantial incomes have greatly reduced federal income tax liabilities, or even no federal income tax liability at all, due to collecting income from sources that are given special tax treatment and using tax deductions and credits. Congress established the *alternative minimum tax* (AMT) to prevent these taxpayers from avoiding the payment of at least some minimum amount of federal income tax.

Although the AMT was initially designed to tax wealthier taxpayers who had managed to use certain deductions and other tax provisions to greatly reduce or eliminate their federal income tax burdens, because there have been few adjustments in the AMT provisions since their inception, inflation has pushed earnings up to the level that more and more taxpayers have become affected by the tax. Therefore, taxpayers with significant itemized deductions or other write-offs would be wise to obtain a Form 6251—the form used to calculate AMT—and work through it to determine whether they are subject to AMT. Failure to include AMT calculations and pay the tax when it is applicable will generally result merely in a letter from the IRS explaining that the tax is due and demanding payment, but it will also include a demand for interest, if not penalty, payments as well.

AUDIT ALERT

Failure to include AMT calculations and pay the tax when it is applicable will generally result in a letter from the IRS explaining that the tax is due and demanding payment, as opposed to an audit letter.

Self-Employment Taxes

Employees are required to pay taxes under provisions of the *Federal Insurance Contributions Act* (FICA). The taxes consist of payments for *old age, survivors, and disability insurance* (OASDI), generally referred to as *Social Security tax*, which is 6.2% of the income subject to the tax, and hospital insurance, known as *Medicare*, which is 1.45% of the income that is subject to the tax. Employers are required to pay FICA taxes on behalf of their employees that are equal to the amount that their employees must pay. As a result, both the employer and employee will be required to pay a total of 7.65% each on the amount of the employee's earnings that are subject to both the OASDI and Medicare components of FICA taxes, for a combined total of 15.3%. Their combined Medicare tax payments on income in excess of the earnings subject to OASDI is 2.9%.

Self-employed taxpayers are required to pay self-employment taxes in lieu of FICA taxes. Since there is no employer to pay a matching share, the nominal rate for self-employment taxes is set at the total of the combined employer's and employee's share of FICA taxes. In an effort to escape the burdensome self-employment tax, some self-employed taxpayers attempt to report their incomes from self-employment as if the earnings were from investments or some other source that is not subject to the tax. Therefore, IRS auditors keep a vigilant watch for such misreporting.

AUDIT ALERT

IRS auditors keep a vigilant watch for self-employed taxpayers attempting to report their self-employment income as if the earnings were from investments or some other source that is not subject to self-employment tax.

Tax Credits

Once a taxpayer has determined his or her tax liability, that liability can be offset dollar-for-dollar by any tax credits to which the party is entitled. There are a number of personal credits for individuals—such as Household and Dependent Care Credit, the Hope and Lifetime Learning Credits, Earned Income Credit, Child Tax Credit, and Child and Dependent Care Expenses Credit—that provide significant tax relief to a number of taxpayers.

All of the various credits have their own specific requirements and limitations that taxpayers must carefully follow in order to be allowed to take them. The IRS routinely subjects returns to an automated review to confirm each taxpayer's entitlement to credits that were claimed.

The withholding taxes held out of a taxpayer's earnings and paid to the U.S. Treasury and estimated tax payments that are paid directly to the IRS by taxpayers are regarded as a form of credit when tax returns are prepared. If a taxpayer overpays his or her taxes through withholdings or estimated payments, those overpayments are refundable to the taxpayer, as are some, but not all, of the other types of credits that are available. If a taxpayer has underpaid his or her federal taxes, payment of the shortfall is due by the filing deadline. However, even if a taxpayer is unable to pay any taxes due, a timely return should still be filed, since failure to file a required return is a criminal offense, whereas failure to pay taxes when they are due is not a crime.

SECTION II

AUDIT ESSENTIALS

No one wants to be audited by the IRS. Even taxpayers who are certain that their returns were accurate and all of their deductions and other tax write-offs justified are somewhat intimidated by the receipt of notice from the IRS that they have been selected for an audit. Being prevailed upon to offer proof of income, deductions, exemptions, and credits, and knowing that there is always the possibility that such proof may be missing or inadequate, or that there may be a disagreement between the taxpayer and IRS auditor over whether a certain receipt constitutes taxable income or whether a write-off or credit is allowable, can be unnerving.

The best way to overcome your fear of tax audits is to educate yourself concerning the types, purposes, and processes of the various IRS audits, how to prepare for an audit, and what it is that is likely to cause you to be selected for an audit. The purpose of this section is to provide you with that information.

Chapter Five
The Audit Process

Only a relatively small number of tax returns are singled out for an actual audit each year. A review of IRS records for the last fifteen years reveals that for most years, between 0.5% and 2% of all of the returns filed were audited.

Under provisions of I.R.C. §6501, the IRS normally has three years from the last day upon which the return was due to audit a return that was filed on time. It does not matter how much earlier than the deadline that a return was filed, since §6501 provides that all returns that were filed on time shall be deemed to have been filed on the last permissible date for purposes of establishing the start of the three-year statute of limitations available to the IRS for auditing returns. If it can be shown that a taxpayer has omitted over 25% of his or her gross income from a tax return for the year, §6501(e)(1)(A) allows the IRS six years to audit and assess additional taxes against the party. When taxpayers file false returns or fail to file required returns, §6501 imposes no time limit on the IRS to audit the taxpayers and assess taxes against them.

The procedure used in carrying out an audit will depend entirely on the type of audit that the IRS chooses to conduct. Each of the various types of audits has a regimen that IRS auditors are trained to follow. Individual auditors are afforded some latitude in choosing the specific approaches to use in conducting a particular type of audit, but if you are selected for an audit, you can expect the general frameworks that follow to apply.

The Letter Audit

All returns are reviewed to some extent when they are processed at the IRS service center where they are filed. Initially, returns are checked for completeness. If required schedules are missing or forms are filed without including necessary Social Security numbers or with missing signatures, taxpayers are notified of their deficiencies and instructed as to how to correct them. Returns that arrive complete, or are subsequently completed if they arrive with deficiencies, are then run through the *Automatic Data Processing* (ADP) computer program, which compares the figures on the return with information, such as 1099s, K-1s, and W-2s, supplied by employers and other third parties. The ADP program also checks returns for math errors. There is also an *Unallowable Items* program that reviews all returns to see if deductions were taken for any items for which deductions are not allowed, such as a deduction for personal credit card interest.

If discrepancies are detected in any of these processes, a letter is sent to the taxpayer informing the party of mistakes on the return that were detected when it was processed at the IRS service center where it was filed. The letter then explains how the party's tax liability is affected by the mistakes and states that either credit will be given for mistakes made in favor of the IRS, which will result in a refund if no other taxes are owed, or the party will be required to pay additional taxes when correction of mistakes increases the tax liability. Interest will also be added to any tax deficiencies assessed.

This *correspondence audit*, or *letter audit* as it is often called, is by far the most common type of IRS audit. Such audits do not require a face-to-face meeting with an IRS auditor; however, the letters cannot be ignored. Taxpayers who agree with the IRS findings that are described in the letter are required to do nothing more than merely pay any tax deficiencies and interest that are demanded. On the other hand, taxpayers who disagree with what the IRS states in its letter must respond with an explanation within the allotted time period, or the proposed additional taxes will be assessed and the taxpayer will be obligated to pay them.

Taxpayers who receive a demand for additional taxes as a result of a letter audit often feel that, since the demand has come directly from the IRS, the determination must be accurate and that they, undoubtedly, owe additional taxes. That is not always the case. The clerical workers that key in data from the millions of tax returns that they process sometimes make mistakes, and there are times when the IRS computer program does not properly process the data. For example, if a taxpayer with three accounts at a single bank, who has received a Form 1099 reporting interest income from each account, were to combine the interest from the three accounts and report the total as a single figure for interest income from that bank, an IRS program set to look for reported interest from three accounts might generate a deficiency notice when it did not locate three separate entries, despite the fact that the interest income from all three accounts was fully reported on the taxpayer's return, but in a form that the computer was not programmed to recognize. Therefore, taxpayers who get letter audit notices that they owe more taxes should carefully review them and verify their accuracy, rather than blindly comply with them.

Taxpayers who believe that they do not owe the additional taxes claimed by the IRS in a letter audit should, in a timely manner, send a letter of their own to the IRS detailing the reasons that they disagree with

TIP—

If you receive a letter audit notice that you owe more in taxes, carefully review it and verify its accuracy.

the findings of the audit. The more thoroughly a taxpayer explains why the IRS is in error, the more likely the matter is to be resolved by that single reply. The letter that the IRS sends to taxpayers as a result of the letter audit will provide an address to which the taxpayer is to send a reply in the event that the demand for more taxes is disputed. Those letters also usually include a telephone number for taxpayers to respond by calling the IRS, but it is usually difficult to get through, and often when callers do get through to someone, they are simply told to submit a written response to the letter that they have received. Any response that is sent to the IRS should include a copy of the letter the IRS sent to the taxpayer in order to ensure that the response is linked to the audit letter.

The Office Audit

Office audits are the lowest level of face-to-face audit conducted by the IRS. This type of audit is initiated with a letter to the taxpayer stating that the party has been selected for an audit, what years are being audited, what books and records to bring, where and when to go for the audit, and the name of the tax examiner to see. There is usually a contact telephone number so that taxpayers may call to clarify instructions or ask to reschedule the audit time in the event that there is a conflict. Unlike the general IRS telephone numbers that are usually supplied to taxpayers in correspondence resulting from letter audits, the telephone numbers contained in notices of office audits are for a local IRS office that handles nothing but audits for a given locale, and the call volume is sufficiently small. Callers will not generally have a great deal of trouble reaching IRS personnel there. Tax examiners are usually willing to reschedule audit times as long as taxpayers are reasonable and do not keep postponing their audits an inordinate number of times.

Upon receipt of a notice of an office audit, a taxpayer should set about gathering up all of the records that the auditor has requested. Typically, the records that are requested will be very broad in their scope. It is not uncommon for a tax examiner's notice to include a request for all books and records used in preparation of the taxpayer's tax return for a certain year, including all supporting documentation for all deductions taken. They often specifically request all bank records for the year in question, even if no deposits or payments affecting the taxpayer's taxable income were made from those accounts. This will often even include dormant accounts. The purpose behind such a broad request for bank records is to allow the tax examiner to verify that the taxpayer has not used an account to hide income.

Taxpayers who do not wish to deal with the examiners on their own have the right to send a representative in their place. The party that they choose must generally be an attorney, a CPA, someone enrolled to practice before the IRS (referred to as an *enrolled agent)*, or a party who was paid to prepare the return that is the subject of the audit. Sending a competent representative to an office audit in their place is the only sensible response a taxpayer can make to a notice of an office audit.

Tax examiners, although not required to have a degree in accounting, must have a certain minimum number of hours of accounting courses and undergo extensive training in how to audit tax returns. Therefore, individuals who represent themselves in office audits are usually overmatched by the tax examiner as far as relevant education is concerned. Furthermore, the tax examiner will have vastly more experience in being involved in tax audits. Tax professionals who represent clients in audits are often significantly better

TIP—

Sending a competent representative to an office audit in your place is the only sensible response you can make to a notice of an office audit.

educated concerning accounting and tax issues than the tax examiners that they deal with, and they usually have significant experience in dealing with IRS audits.

Another advantage to engaging the services of a tax professional to respond to a notice of an office audit is that the competent and experienced representative may well be able to anticipate what has triggered the audit and better respond to the tax examiner's inquiries during the audit. Sometimes tax examiners will word their requests for documentation in the initial audit notice in a way that will tip off an experienced tax professional as to the direction in which the tax examiner will likely proceed. For instance, a request for all books and records in general that is accompanied by a specific request for certain records, such as business travel expenses or charitable contributions, is a good indicator that those specific areas are the ones of major concern.

The most effective tax professionals who represent taxpayers at audits will do a pre-audit before ever going before a tax examiner. In the pre-audit, the representative will review the taxpayer's books and records from the perspective of the tax examiner. If he or she has ideas as to what the main areas of interest to the examiner are, he or she will devote particular attention to those issues.

Even merely sorting out receipts, checks, bank statements, and other records, adding them up on an adding machine that generates a paper tape, and attaching that tape to the items that were totaled, and then organizing those items so that they can be quickly produced when they are requested by a tax examiner, will be instrumental in the representative creating the impression that the taxpayer has kept good

TIP—

A request for all books and records in general that is accompanied by a specific request for certain records, such as business travel expenses or charitable contributions, is a good indicator that those specific areas are the ones of major concern.

records and complied with the tax laws. Nothing will bring a tax audit to a rapid conclusion any more quickly than an immediate production of supporting documentation in response to an auditor's request for it. If you choose to do an office audit on your own, you should take the same steps of organizing your records in a manner that will allow for the quickest and easiest production of the material to the auditor.

Still another advantage to taxpayers of having a representative respond to a notice of an office audit is that the taxpayer does not generally have to attend the audit at all. Occasionally, an auditor may insist on interviewing a taxpayer at the beginning of the audit. The scope of such interviews should be restricted to general questions, such as the type of employment that the taxpayer has, the number of dependents in the household, along with information as to how those dependents are related to the taxpayer and how much of the year they reside with the taxpayer, whether the taxpayer belongs to a *barter club* (more about this later), how much cash the party had at the beginning and end of the tax year, and whether all of the taxpayer's income is deposited in a bank account. Before a representative agrees to have his or her client appear for an initial interview, he or she should make it clear to the auditor that there will be no discussion with the client concerning specific matters related to the client's tax returns during the interview, and should be prepared to call a halt to the interview in the event that the auditor disregards that stipulation during the interview.

Furthermore, prior to an initial interview with his or her client, representatives should counsel their clients to answer

TIP—

If you choose to do an office audit on your own, sort out receipts, checks, bank statements, and other records, add them up on an adding machine that generates a paper tape, attach that tape to the items, and organize everything so that they can be quickly produced for the auditor.

questions briefly and to the point, and to refuse to answer questions if advised to do so by their representative. It is imperative that taxpayers follow their representative's instructions concerning their conduct during such interviews. However, if a taxpayer finds him- or herself in a situation in which an auditor has turned an initial interview into an actual audit of his or her return, and the party's representative is not assertive enough to object and end the process, the taxpayer should be prepared to refuse to further participate and point out to the auditor, as well as the representative, that the reason that the representative was hired was to respond to the auditor in his or her place.

One of the biggest advantages to taxpayers in having a professional representative sit in for them for a tax audit is that when the auditor brings up unexpected issues and begins to ask questions relevant to them, the representative can honestly plead ignorance and offer to find out what the answers are from the taxpayer. This gives the representative and the taxpayer time to deliberate and contemplate the relevance of the information to the taxpayer's income as it was reported on the return that is under scrutiny. Also, this prevents taxpayers from giving offhand answers to questions, such as those concerning average household expenses, that may be seriously inaccurate, but that the auditor may subsequently use to substantiate an assertion that the taxpayer had understated his or her income, since the reported income was not large enough to cover those expenses. Later attempts to correct initial estimates with lower, but accurate, figures are often met with considerable resistance from tax auditors.

TIP —

One of your biggest advantages in having a professional representative sit in for you for a tax audit is that when the auditor brings up unexpected issues and begins to ask questions, the representative can honestly plead ignorance and offer to find out what the answers are later from you.

Therefore, it is important to supply accurate responses to auditors' questions in the first place.

Before a taxpayer can be represented in an audit by another person, the party being audited must execute a Form 2848, Power of Attorney, granting the representative the authority to represent the taxpayer. The form must specify the type of audit the representative has authority to represent the taxpayer in, such as an audit of Form 1040, and the year or years for which the authority is granted. The form must be signed by the party being represented, and if a joint return is involved, both spouses must sign the Form 2848.

The Field Audit

Field audits are a more serious level of audit than office audits. In such audits, tax examiners, who are generally referred to as *field auditors*, go to the taxpayer's home or business in order to conduct the audit. In so doing, this gives the auditor much greater access to the books and records of the taxpayer. Field auditors are generally better educated and more experienced than their counterparts who conduct office audits. In essence, field auditors are the elite among IRS auditors. This is a primary reason that, while it is extremely advisable for taxpayers to engage the services of a tax professional to appear in their place in an office audit, it is absolutely essential that taxpayers who are subjected to a field audit get a competent representative to appear on their behalf at the audit.

Since field auditors go to the taxpayer to conduct the audit, rather than having the party bring in certain requested

TIP—

In most cases, it is advisable that if you are being subjected to a field audit, you leave the premises during the time that the field auditor is present.

information, as is the case in an office audit, the scope of a field audit is virtually unlimited. Going to a taxpayer's home or place of business gives the auditor an opportunity to observe such things as the area devoted to an in-home office or the activities going on at a business. These observations may cause the auditor to question certain deductions or to expand the audit into new areas.

As with the office audit, taxpayers who have chosen to have a qualified person represent them in a field audit may choose not to participate directly with the IRS auditor in the actual audit process. In fact, that is exactly what they should choose to do. In most cases, it is advisable for the taxpayer who is being subjected to a field audit to leave the premises during the time that the field auditor is present. In so doing, whenever the auditor has questions, it will be easier for the representative to postpone answering questions that should have more time spent considering the various ramifications of those lines of inquiry, since the taxpayer is not immediately available. Also, with less activity going on around the auditor, he or she is less likely to be inspired to expand the scope of the audit.

Personal representatives are appointed for field audits using the same Form 2848 that taxpayers use to appoint representatives for office audits. The same group of people who qualify to represent taxpayers in office audits are also permitted to represent clients in field audits. However, since field audits are generally more serious and more extensive than office audits, and the auditors are better qualified, it would be advisable for a taxpayer who has received notice of a field audit to engage the services of one of the more qualified parties among the group of those who are permitted to represent taxpayers in audits.

TIP —

Making false statements to a U.S. tax auditor is a federal crime.

Furthermore, taxpayers who have been selected for a field audit need to go ahead and engage the services of a representative from the very beginning. It is simply a very bad idea to start out representing oneself with the idea in mind that it would be best to wait until the going gets rough before hiring a representative. Even in the initial meeting, a taxpayer may make comments or give statements to the auditor that a subsequent representative simply cannot overcome, or a resentful taxpayer's attitude may so alienate the auditor that he or she becomes determined to find some sort of taxpayer error that will lead to a deficiency. Even worse, the taxpayer may attempt to cover up a tax deficiency by lying to the auditor, and making false statements to a U.S. tax auditor is a federal crime.

Chapter Six

IRS Approaches to Audits

Tax examiners and field auditors are allowed some latitude in choosing how to carry out their assigned audits, but they are trained to use certain basic approaches and they will have to answer to their supervisors if they fail to use one of the preferred methods for auditing a taxpayer's return. Following are brief explanations of the more popular audit techniques employed by IRS auditors.

The Bank Deposits Method

The most fundamental approach taken by the IRS in audits is the *bank deposits method*. The income of the taxpayer being audited is verified by adding up all deposits in all of the party's accounts in banks, credit unions, and brokerage houses. That total, along with any cash receipts that the taxpayer acknowledges having received, is then compared to the amount of income shown on the taxpayer's return. In order to perform an audit using the bank deposits method, it is essential that the auditor have all of the taxpayer's deposits to enter into the calculations. This is why auditors generally request all of a taxpayer's bank records, even though no deposits may have been made in some of them, or some of the accounts may have been completely dormant. If the taxpayer's deposits and admitted cash receipts exceed the reported income, the party will be assessed a tax deficiency for the difference, unless it can be shown that the difference was from a nontaxed source, such as gifts or a hoard of cash that was accumulated from prior years.

The reason that auditors routinely ask taxpayers how much cash they had at the beginning and at the end of the tax year is to establish the net change in cash for the year that is to then be added or subtracted, as the case may be, from the total of the taxpayer's deposits and admitted cash expenditures. Also, by quizzing a taxpayer concerning the amount of cash that he or she had at the beginning of the tax year, the auditor is looking for inconsistent statements to later negate a *cash hoard defense*. If a taxpayer tries to explain away a tax deficiency by claiming to have used money from a cash hoard that had been accumulated in previous years, but the party had previously indicated that he or she had not had any appreciable amount of cash at the beginning of the year, this inconsistency in the taxpayer's statements will likely render the party's cash hoard defense ineffective.

Such a situation further points out the wisdom of having a tax professional represent taxpayers in audits. Most taxpayers are reluctant to admit having a cash hoard, especially if it was obtained in the form of cash income that may have previously been inadvertently unreported, even if the statute of limitations protects them from action by the IRS. However, if a tax professional engaged to represent a taxpayer in an audit were to discover the deficiency by doing a preliminary audit using the bank deposits method, and confront the taxpayer who then admitted to the cash hoard, the representative would know to advise the client to admit the existence of the cash hoard at the inception of the audit. Then, the taxpayer would be able to explain that some of his or her funds that were spent during the year for which the party's tax return is being audited were from a source that was either previously taxed or that the IRS can no longer tax.

Once an auditor uses the bank deposits method to reconcile bank deposits and cash receipts with reported income, the next step is to address the validity of the deductions that were taken on the return. That process will generally start with the auditor requesting proof of the claimed expenditures. Any expenditure that cannot be supported by a cancelled check or receipt of some kind will likely be disallowed. The auditor may also challenge even some of the deductions that were substantiated. Business-related expenses are especially likely to attract the attention of auditors. They will ask questions about deductions taken for them in an effort to ascertain whether or not the expenses were ordinary and necessary for the taxpayer's business. This will include a determination of whether or not the expenditures were extravagant, and a determination as to whether or not the taxpayer has included nondeductible personal expenses among his or her business expenses. (See Chapter 7 for more on business-related expenses.) In addition to various questions concerning the nature of deductions that were taken, by the taxpayer, auditors usually review mileage logs and notes concerning the purpose of business meetings for which a deduction for meals was taken, as part of the verification process.

The biggest shortcoming of the bank deposits method of audit is that it does not detect cash receipts that were collected and neither deposited nor spent on deductible items, unless the taxpayer admits to their receipt. However, this technique will likely detect taxpayers who underreport their income simply because they made mistakes in completing their return or due to inaccurate bookkeeping, or who are deliberately attempting to evade their tax liabilities, but are very unsophisticated in their efforts. It should also expose taxpayers who have overstated their deductions and expenses or who have taken deductions for nondeductible expenditures.

Indirect Methods of Establishing Income —Using Earnings to Reconstruct Income

Whenever a taxpayer is suspected of deliberately concealing income by failing to deposit receipts in a bank or other financial institution, IRS auditors can approach their audit of the party from one of two indirect methods. The auditors may attempt to reconstruct the party's income and show that the party failed to fully report earnings, or they may attempt to total all of the party's net worth, and show that it exceeded reported income.

If a taxpayer earns income in a manner such that sizable amounts of it come from a single source, reconstruction of the party's income may prove to be a practical option. This method will work best for IRS auditors when there is some record that can be used to establish that a taxpayer had unreported earnings. Sometimes those records even reveal how much the party actually or probably earned.

EXAMPLE:

Lee, a trial lawyer, was suspected of failing to report all of his income for the year. IRS auditors were able to use the local court records to determine what cases he had handled during the year, and contacted his clients to see how much each had paid him in fees and approximately when those payments were made. The auditors were then able to compare the information received from the clients to Lee's bank statements in order to determine which of those payments had not been reported.

EXAMPLE:
Saumil had a job as a billing clerk making $24,000 annually. He worked on weekends as a self-employed security guard at a flea market and was paid $100 per week in cash. When the flea market operator was audited, he told the auditor that the $5,200 deduction that he had taken for security on his Schedule C was for the money that he had paid Saumil. Upon reviewing Saumil's return, the auditor discovered that he had reported only the $24,000 salary that had been shown on his Form W-2. The auditor will undoubtedly expand his audit to include Saumil, and will easily be able to show that Saumil failed to report his self-employment earnings.

If small transactions that are conducted in cash are a taxpayer's typical transaction, IRS auditors may not be able to reconstruct the taxpayer's income unless they can develop a creative approach. In such situations, auditors may attempt to establish a taxpayer's income through detective work, such as observing a suspected tax evader's place of business in order to determine about how many customers he or she has per day, what the average sale is, and about what percentage of profit was made on each sale. The auditor would then contend that by compiling such data for a week, and multiplying it by 52, he or she could establish the taxpayer's true earnings. It would then be up to the taxpayer to show that the business was seasonal and the auditor had chosen an especially busy week to observe, or that business had dramatically increased compared to the level for prior years for which returns were being audited.

Skilled auditors will anticipate these defenses and will ask questions about the nature of the business, whether or not it is seasonal, and whether the volume of business has changed significantly throughout the years up to the current date. By establishing a record of the taxpayer's answers to these questions before spending time observing the party's business, subsequent attempts to refute the auditor's findings by changing prior answers are not likely to be very persuasive. There are a number of variations involving the approach of reconstructing a taxpayer's income on the basis of data collected by an auditor.

EXAMPLE:

Punjab owns and operates a convenience store. He reported his income from the store as $36,000 for the year. Records of Punjab's purchases from his suppliers indicate that he bought $105,000 worth of cigarettes during the year, $156,000 worth of beer, $212,000 worth of gasoline, and $54,000 worth of other miscellaneous items. By looking at the prices that he charges for goods in his store, it was determined that his markup on cigarettes is 25%, his markup on beer is 30%, his markup on gasoline is 10%, and his markup on everything else is 50%. Using these percentages and applying them to Punjab's purchases for the year, the auditor could determine that his gross profits were $26,250 from cigarettes, $46,800 from beer, $21,200 from gasoline, and $27,000 from miscellaneous items, for a total of $121,250. The total of Punjab's expenses associated with the store were $64,200, as reported on his Schedule C of Form 1040 and verified by the

auditor. Therefore, Punjab's net income from the store was actually $57,050, so the $36,000 net income reported on his return was understated by $21,050.

Indirect Methods of Establishing Income—Using Expenditures Plus Increase in Net Worth to Determine Income

When reconstructing a taxpayer's income is not practical, but the party is suspected of failing to report some income, IRS auditors may attempt to determine the accurate total income by adding up all expenditures plus any increase in net worth. Some expenses— such as home mortgage payments, car note, utility bills, and insurance payments—are readily ascertainable. Expenditures for food, clothing, and entertainment are usually more difficult to determine, although in many cases, interviews with the taxpayer or the party's representative may give the auditor some of that information. Alternatively, the auditor may simply use an average for such expenditures for similarly situated taxpayers. In some of the more drastic cases, agents have followed taxpayers, observed their spending habits, and questioned merchants about the parties' past purchases. Once a party's monthly expenditures are calculated for the entire year, major purchases that were not bought on credit are added to

TIP—

The IRS anticipates that if you are attempting to cover up tax evasion, you will claim to have supplemented your spending from a cash hoard rather than from gifts that cannot be substantiated.

them, along with increases in savings and checking accounts and investment in securities or other assets. This total is then compared to the party's reported income.

If a party's reported income falls short of the total of his or her expenditures plus net increase in assets, the taxpayer must then show a nontaxable source for the shortfall in order to avoid being assessed for additional taxes along with interest and penalties on the difference, or perhaps even prosecuted on criminal charges for tax evasion. If such a taxpayer claims to have obtained funds from a gift as a nontaxable source, auditors will then question the donor and demand documentation of the gifts, such as cancelled checks or proof of withdrawal of funds that were used to make the gifts. Therefore, the IRS anticipates that most taxpayers who are attempting to cover up tax evasion will claim to have supplemented their spending from a cash hoard rather than from gifts that cannot be substantiated.

The IRS Response to the Cash Hoard Defense

It is not terribly uncommon for taxpayers who are found to have a tax deficiency as a result of an audit (using either the bank deposits method or reconstruction of income using expenditures plus increase in net worth method) to claim that their unreported income is nontaxable, since it came from a previously accumulated cash hoard. As previously mentioned, such defenses are anticipated by IRS auditors, and they question taxpayers, either directly or through their representatives, concerning how much cash the taxpayer had at the beginning of

TIP—

The IRS will use the denial of a cash hoard against you if you later attempt to assert the cash hoard defense (even when it is legitimate).

the tax year. This is done to establish that they had little or no cash hoarded and forestall assertion of the cash hoard defense at the conclusion of the audit.

Since the term *cash hoard* has an almost sinister tone to it, and since admission of the existence of a cash hoard may seem tantamount to an admission of prior underpayment of taxes, most taxpayers are prone to deny the existence of a cash hoard upon initial questioning. The IRS will use that denial against them if they later attempt to legitimately assert the cash hoard defense.

Even when taxpayers have admitted to the existence of a cash hoard at the inception of the audit and subsequently respond to added tax assessments or charges of tax evasion by asserting the tax hoard defense, the IRS will likely challenge the taxpayer's use of the defense. The most common approach of IRS auditors dealing with tax evaders who claim to have drawn from a cash hoard as a nontaxable source to supplement their spending is to show that the argument is inconsistent with the party's behavior and financial history. If it can be shown that the taxpayer had borrowed money in order to make purchases, that property bought on credit had been repossessed in the not too distant past, or that the party had filed bankruptcy fairly recently, these results would be totally inconsistent with what would be expected from a taxpayer with a sizable cash hoard. If the taxpayer argues that the cash hoard had been accumulated since such an event, the auditor will simply audit all of the party's returns back to the year of the event to show that the party had spent what he or she had earned. Such audits would be permissible for that purpose, even though the years involved may be too far back to permit the IRS to assess taxes for understatements of income that are discovered.

TIP—

Audits of returns in which too much time has past to have a tax deficiency accessed can still occur to prove a pattern of spending habits for a current audit.

Chapter Seven

Circumstances that are Most Likely to Cause an Audit

The IRS, by virtue of the dictates of I.R.C. §6103, is required not to disclose the methodology for selecting returns for audit. However, experience and testimony of various IRS officials before Congress over the years have given some reliable data concerning IRS audit selection criteria. There are any number of circumstances that can trigger an IRS audit, some of which are relatively unique.

For example, a couple in the northeastern U.S. was selected for audit when they caught the attention of an IRS auditor as he ate lunch, when they pulled up to the same restaurant driving a new Rolls Royce convertible. Because it was so unusual for someone in that small town to have such an expensive car, the auditor got their license number, traced the identity of the owners, and started an audit that eventually led to their conviction for federal income tax evasion. Likewise, it is not unusual for news stories that detail the arrest of suspects in possession of large sums of cash to attract the interest of IRS auditors.

However, rather than being triggered by some unusual event, most audits result from rather mundane circumstances. The following are among the most common situations that will cause the IRS to select a taxpayer for an audit.

Income from Self-Employment

Among those more likely to be audited than average are the self-employed. The reason that the self-employed are targets for audits is that they have more opportunities to conceal their income through underreporting and taking excess deductions for expenses than do those who work for wages and salaries. Those whose self-employment activities normally generate significant amounts of cash receipts are among the more likely of the self-employed to be audited. Owners of convenience stores, restaurants, and bars are prime examples of taxpayers who fall into this category, as are a host of other owners of small businesses.

Self-employed taxpayers whose businesses do not generate significant cash receipts are still more likely to be audited than employees who earn their incomes in the form of wages and salaries. While self-employed taxpayers who do little cash business may find it more difficult to conceal receipts, it is still possible to do so by cashing checks received in payment for goods and services, rather than depositing them. Although it requires some effort on the part of IRS auditors, they can detect this practice by reviewing the cancelled checks of a self-employed taxpayer's customers to see if they were endorsed for deposit or were cashed, by reviewing the taxpayer's own records to see if any checks that were cashed were later returned for insufficient funds and credited against the party's account, and by questioning tellers at the taxpayer's bank to see if they remember instances in which the taxpayer cashed checks rather than depositing them.

Some self-employed parties have even been known to engage in elaborate schemes in which they write checks to fictitious employees, subcontractors,

> **TIP—**
>
> Although it requires some effort on the part of IRS auditors, they can detect self-employed individuals who cash checks instead of depositing them through a number of methods.

or suppliers, and then pose as those parties and negotiate the checks themselves. Such schemes create tax deductions for the taxpayer, which reduce the party's taxable self-employment income, without having to actually part with the money. Auditors who suspect such a scam may insist on interviewing the taxpayer's employees, subcontractors, and other recipients of payments.

Most self-employed taxpayers do not go to such lengths as creating fictitious employees and other recipients in order to generate deductible expenses. However, it is not uncommon for self-employed taxpayers to either overstate the size of their legitimate deductions or to take a deduction for expenses that are not deductible. The IRS is keenly aware of the potential for taxpayers to use inflated or bogus deductions in an effort to reduce their tax liabilities, and have developed ways to detect the practices.

The IRS has compiled profiles of the typical income and deduction expenses for various businesses. These profiles are reflected in a computer program that the IRS runs returns through for a comparison with what has been typical for similarly situated taxpayers in the past. The more that a return differs from what is normal, the more likely the IRS is to audit the return. Although the IRS does not publish this information, IRS practice indicates that as a general rule, self-employed taxpayers who hold their deductible expenses on Schedule C to no more than about half of their gross income from their trade or business are much less likely to be audited than those whose expenses are a somewhat higher percentage of gross income. Self-employed taxpayers whose expenses are two-thirds or more of their gross income are likely to be audited.

In some instances, the IRS has developed more refined statistical data concerning the typical business in a particular industry, and rather than using the general guideline of auditing businesses whose expenses are

TIP—

Self-employed taxpayers whose expenses are two-thirds or more of their gross income are likely to be audited.

two-thirds or more of their gross income, they will use the statistics that are unique to that industry. As a result, businesses whose deductible expenses are less than two-thirds of their gross income, but whose expenses are still well above the norm for their industry, may still be singled out for audit on the basis of abnormally high expense deductions, just as a business with deductible expenses that exceed two-thirds of its gross income may not be selected for audit when its industry is characterized by a high ratio of expenses to gross revenue.

For example, if the owner of a Mexican fast food restaurant were to take a deduction for the food that he bought that was equal to 30% of his gross income, but the IRS had determined from its audits of such businesses over past years that the typical Mexican fast foot restaurant's cost of raw food used in its operation has been 22% of its gross revenue, the owner that took a deduction of 30% would appear to be a likely candidate for audit. This would be due to an excessive deduction for food costs, even if his overall deductions were less than the two-thirds total that triggers an audit for businesses in general. During the course of that audit (if he were selected for one) the taxpayer should be able to satisfy that auditor by showing that, in an effort to be more competitive, he priced his menu items lower than other Mexican restaurants, used more coupons or other forms of discounts than his competitors, or bought higher quality raw food in hopes that it would result in a higher quality finished product that would bring customers back for more.

Taxpayers who have fabricated their tax deductions by padding their legitimate business expenses will be caught, in the event of an audit, when they cannot produce records to support the full amount of their deductions. They can likely

TIP—

Using refined statistical data, the IRS can detect if you are claiming expenses above the industry standard, which often results in an audit.

avoid criminal prosecution by claiming that they merely made a math error, but they will still be liable for a tax deficiency plus interest and penalties. Also, when an auditor finds a significant overstatement of expense deductions in a given year, he or she may very well decide to expand the audit, and go back as many additional years as the IRS is permitted to, in order to check for such math errors in those years, as well.

Rather than making an out-and-out overstatement of their business expenses, it is not uncommon for some self-employed taxpayers to use their business account to pay nondeductible personal expenses, and then take a deduction for them as if they were legitimate business expenses. In such cases, since taxpayers will have documentation to support their deductions, auditors will have to go beyond merely verifying proof of the expenditures in order to detect the impropriety of the deduction, and they are trained to do so.

Once auditors verify that a taxpayer has actually made an expenditure for a deduction that was claimed, they then usually want to scrutinize the party's records that support the deductibility of the payment. For example, unless a vehicle was used exclusively for business use, a taxpayer must support his or her auto expense deduction with a log book that shows business usage of the vehicle. Likewise, business deductions for meals and entertainment must be supported by a record of the nature of the business that was conducted in connection with the expenditures, although as little as a notation by the taxpayer on the backs of the receipts will suffice.

An auditor who suspects that a taxpayer has fabricated a business purpose for travel or meals and entertainment may require that the party obtain an affidavit from the client who was called on or taken out to

TIP—

IRS auditors are trained to spot when nondeductible personal expenses are being claimed as legitimate business deductions.

eat and entertained, which verifies that the taxpayer made the calls on the client or took him or her out to eat or out for entertainment for a business purpose. In some cases, the auditor may even choose to interview a taxpayer's clients in order to verify claimed expenditures for travel or meals and entertainment. Even if a taxpayer's clients verify that they were taken out for meals and entertainment, the auditor may elect to go further by interviewing the taxpayer and his or her clients concerning the nature of the business discussions, who was present, and the setting in which the discussions took place, and then applying the rules that govern the deductibility of such expenses. The auditor will then disallow the deduction if the discussions were not *directly related to* or *associated with* the taxpayer's business, as is required by law in order for the expense to be deductible. An auditor would also seek to disallow a deduction for meals and entertainment to the degree that it included expenditures for mere companions of taxpayers or their clients, or to the degree that the expenditures were extravagant.

Auditors can always challenge the deductibility of an expense on the basis that it is not an ordinary and necessary business expense. (see Chapter 2.) Such challenges are most likely when the taxpayer receives some degree of personal benefit from the expenditure, as he or she would from entertainment of a client, or when the expenditure is extravagant.

The IRS has limited resources with which to cover the costs of audits. Therefore, it only makes sense that among the primary criteria for selecting taxpayers for audit should be the potential for recovering additional taxes from them. This is another significant reason why self-employed taxpayers are more likely to be audited than those who are not self-employed, since any increases in net

TIP—

Auditors can always challenge the deductibility of an expense, and are most likely to do so when you receive some degree of personal benefit from the expenditure.

taxable income found as the result of an audit will not only increase the taxpayer's federal income tax liability, but will also increase the self-employment tax on the party's self-employment income.

Using the Services of Independent Contractors

Although self-employed taxpayers are more likely to be audited than those who are not self-employed, taxpayers who engage in a trade or business that uses the services of independent contractors are more likely to be audited than those who do not. It is not always clear-cut as to whether a worker is an employee or an independent contractor, and it is this uncertainty that creates an increased potential for audits when workers are classified as independent contractors.

If it is determined that a worker is laboring as another party's employee, the party who has employed the worker must deduct income taxes and taxes imposed by the Federal Insurance Contributions Act (FICA) from the worker's earnings. For most workers, the FICA tax rate is 7.65%. In addition to being required to withhold these taxes and pay them over to the U.S. Treasury, employers are required to pay a matching share of FICA taxes, and also must pay federal unemployment tax on their employees' earnings. Along with the duty to pay taxes on behalf of their employees, there is the additional burden of having to file a quarterly Form 941 to report the FICA and income taxes withheld and paid, and a

TIP—

Self-employed taxpayers are more likely to be audited than those who are not self-employed, since any increases in net taxable income will not only increase the taxpayer's federal income tax liability, but will also increase the party's self-employment tax liability.

quarterly Form 940 to report the unemployment taxes paid by the employer. Furthermore, although it is not a tax, the laws of every state impose the requirement of maintaining workers' compensation insurance on employees, once some minimum number of employees are hired, which may be avoided by using independent contractors to perform work, rather than hiring employees. The premiums for workers' compensation insurance are calculated as a percentage of the wages paid to workers, and that percentage is determined by the hazardousness of the work being performed. Generally, a sizable percentage of the premium must be paid at the inception of the policy, with the balance payable in monthly installments.

The paperwork required of an employer to withhold, pay, and report income taxes and FICA taxes from employees' earnings, and the financial burden of having to pay unemployment taxes, workers' compensation insurance premiums, and a matching amount of FICA taxes, causes many employers to attempt to pass employees off as independent contractors. As a result, the worker, who is treated as an independent contractor, will likely be uncovered by workers' compensation insurance and will be required to pay self-employment tax at the nominal rate of 15.3% on most, if not all, of his or her income, since the worker will have no employer to pay a matching share.

Workers who may not fully understand the consequences of being classified as independent contractors will probably initially be delighted when their employers do not withhold any taxes from their paychecks. However, workers who were misclassified as independent contractors and are faced with large tax deficits due to their employer's failure

Tip—

Workers who believe that they have been misclassified as an independent contractor can report the misclassification to the IRS, which could lead to a full-blown audit of the employer.

to withhold taxes and pay in the employer's share of FICA taxes are likely to be very upset, as are workers who are injured on the job and discover that they are not covered by workers' compensation insurance, and workers who lose their jobs and are turned down for unemployment benefits.

Workers who believe that they were misclassified can file a Form SS-8 with the IRS, requesting that a determination of their employment status be made, or they can go to a local IRS office and report the misclassification, and the employer's practices will be investigated, which could lead to a full-blown audit. Furthermore, if the employer is found to have misclassified the worker who objected to being classified as an independent contractor, the IRS will review the employer's other workers to see if they were also misclassified, and hold the employer liable for all of the misclassifications.

Employers who misclassify employees as independent contractors are not only subject to assessment of considerable tax deficiencies plus penalties and interest, but, if the misclassification is determined to be willful, they will also be subject to criminal charges. Therefore, it is important for employers to carefully consider whether a worker really is an independent contractor before treating the party as such. In order to assist taxpayers in making this determination, the IRS has issued guidelines in the form of a twenty-part test.

Among the twenty factors set forth by the IRS, if the following are answered in the affirmative, it indicates that a worker is an employee.

1. Whether the party for whom a worker is performing services has the right to instruct the worker concerning the details of how the work is performed.
2. Whether the employer provides training for the worker.
3. Whether the worker's services are integrated into the employer's operation.
4. Whether the worker must personally render the services.

5. Whether the employer hires, supervises, and pays any workers who assist the worker whose employment status is in question.
6. Whether the relationship between the worker and employer is continuing.
7. Whether the worker must work set hours.
8. Whether the worker must work full-time for the employer.
9. Whether the worker must perform the services provided on the premises for the employer.
10. Whether the work performed must be done in an order or sequence set by the party for whom the services are done.
11. Whether the worker must submit regular oral or written reports.
12. Whether the worker is paid on an hourly, weekly, or monthly basis, rather than by the job or on commission.
13. Whether the employer pays the worker's business or travel expenses.
14. Whether the employer provides the worker with tools and materials necessary to do the work.
15. Whether the worker has failed to invest in equipment or facilities used to provide the services.
16. Whether either the worker or employer is free to terminate the relationship between them at any time.

Among the twenty factors, an affirmative answer to the following indicates that the worker is an independent contractor.
17. Whether the worker has had to make a significant investment in the facilities used in performing the agreed on work.
18. Whether the worker can either realize a profit or suffer a loss as a result of the performance of the services as agreed.
19. Whether the worker performs services for multiple parties that are not related to one another.
20. Whether the worker's services are made available to the general public.

Owning an Interest in a Partnership or Small Business

Partnerships, as well as corporations that elect Subchapter S status and limited liability companies whose owners elect to have their companies taxed as partnerships, must all file annual tax returns, but the entities pay no taxes. Their returns are filed simply to show the amounts of income or loss generated by the business entity and then attributed, which is referred to as being *passed through*, to the various owners. Despite the fact that such entities do not pay taxes, their returns are still subject to being audited. Since the profits and losses of these businesses affect the level of the incomes of the recipients, who do pay taxes, audits of such organizations are not uncommon. In fact, since any increase in income resulting from an audit of such an entity will result in an increase in the taxable income of every owner, it makes good economic sense for the IRS to devote some of its limited manpower to these types of audits, rather than to audits of individual taxpayers whose incomes were derived solely from wages or salaries.

If an audit of a partnership or small business results in a significant increase in taxable income for the entity, the auditor may decide to expand the scope of the inquiry and audit each of the individual owners as well, since they will generally be the ones who operate their businesses. Plus, the auditor will already have shown that the partners have a propensity, either by carelessness or design, to understate taxable income. Therefore, since an owner may be swept into a personal audit when his or her partnership or small business is chosen for an audit, and may also be chosen on an individual basis, such a party is clearly more likely to be audited than those who are only susceptible to being chosen for an audit on an individual basis.

TIP—

A business owner may be swept into a personal audit when his or her partnership or small business is chosen for an audit.

If an individual is chosen for an audit, and the party owns an interest in a partnership or small business, the auditor may decide to expand the audit to include an audit of the business. Likewise, the auditor may then see merit in taking the audit beyond the business to include the other owners in addition to the one who was initially selected for audit. Therefore, an owner of an interest in a partnership or small business is not only susceptible to being chosen for an audit on an individual basis, but also has the added exposure of becoming a part of the audit of the business of which he or she owns part. He or she may also indirectly become involved in the audit of a fellow owner of the business once the audit of that taxpayer is expanded to include the business and all of its owners.

A Dealer Showing Investment Income in the Items in Which He or She Deals

Income realized from investments is not considered self-employment income. However, income earned by a self-employed party as a *dealer* in goods, commodities, realty, securities, or other items, which may also be commonly held as investments, is a form of self-employment income. A taxpayer with losses from what would typically be an investment benefits from those losses being classified as having come from a trade or business, as would be the case with a dealer, since the losses could be used to offset ordinary income without limit. Losses from investments, known as *capital losses*, can only be used to offset capital gains without limitation and can be used to offset no more than $3,000 of ordinary income per year.

Since most dividend income and gains on the sale of assets that were held for investment for over a year—known as *long-term capital gains*—are subject to a maximum tax rate of 15%, whereas ordinary income may be taxed at income tax rates of up to 35% and are further subjected to either FICA taxes or self-employment taxes, taxpayers who have gains on what are traditionally thought of as investments greatly benefit from being considered to be investors—rather than dealers—in such assets. Therefore, it is very important to distinguish between income in the form of gains and losses from investments and self-employment income, and losses realized by a self-employed dealer from the sale of items typically marketed for investment purposes. There are separate rules for making this determination on the basis of whether the taxpayer is involved in securities, real estate, or generating royalty income.

Securities Dealers

Although the I.R.C. does not define what constitutes a dealer in stocks or securities, Treasury Regulation §1.1402(a)-5(d) does so very well. It states that a dealer in stocks or securities is a merchant of stocks or securities with an established place of business, regularly engaged in the business of purchasing stocks or securities and reselling them to customers. In short, a securities dealer is someone who, as a merchant, buys stocks or securities, and sells them to customers with a view to the gains and profits that may be derived therefrom. Therefore, it appears from the Regulation that in order for a taxpayer to be considered to be a dealer in stocks or securities, potentially causing his or her proceeds from investments to be includible as net earnings from self-employment, the party must be sufficiently involved in that activity that he or she is considered to be conducting a trade or business for the purpose of marketing stocks or securities to the public.

If it is determined that a taxpayer is not a dealer in stocks or other securities, none of the party's income therefrom will be considered

TIP—

It is very important to distinguish between income in the form of gains and losses from investments and self-employment income, and losses realized by a self-employed dealer from the sale of items typically marketed for investment purposes.

to be self-employment income. However, if a taxpayer is deemed to be a securities dealer, the I.R.C. provides that even that party can still realize investment income, rather than self-employment income, from personally speculating in stocks or securities. Internal Revenue Code §1402(a)(3) excludes from the definition of net earnings from self-employment, items that are not "(i) stock in trade or other property of a kind which would properly be includible in inventory if on hand at the close of the tax payable year, nor (ii) property held primarily for sale to customers in the ordinary course of the trade or business." After sorting out the double negatives of this Code provision, it is apparent that the one who is a dealer in stocks and other securities is not only entitled to separate his or her personal investment holdings from stocks or securities held in inventory for sale to customers, but is required to do so. Once the distinction is made between stocks or securities held in inventory and those held by a dealer for speculation or investment, the tax treatment of any gains or losses from their sale is similar to the dealer's tax treatment of interest and dividends that he or she receives from holdings of stocks or securities. Any gains or losses realized by such a dealer on the sale of stocks or securities that were being held for investment or speculation will not be includible in the dealer's self-employment income, but will be regarded as investment income. Income realized on the sale of stocks or securities that were held in inventory would be self-employment income.

Real Estate Dealers

Income from the rental of real estate and gains from sale of realty are excluded from the definition of self-employment income unless the rents or gains from sale of realty are received by a real estate dealer in the course of his or her trade or business. In determining whether or not a taxpayer is a dealer in real estate, Treasury Regulation §1.1402(a)-4(a) provides the following definition.

In general, an individual who is engaged in the business of selling real estate to customers with a view to the gains and profits that may be derived from such sales is a real estate dealer.

On the other hand, an individual who merely holds real estate for investment or speculation and receives rentals therefrom is not considered a real estate dealer.

As with securities dealers, real estate dealers can still realize investment and rental income from real estate that will not be considered to constitute self-employment income. The determination of whether income derived in the form of rents or gains from sale of realty will be treated as investment income or self-employment income will be based on whether the real estate was held for sale to customers in the ordinary course of the taxpayer's trade or business as a real estate dealer, in which case the income derived therefrom is self-employment income. If the property was held for investment or speculation, the income is not self-employment income.

Royalty Income

Royalties are payments received for use of a patent or copyright, or that are derived from oil, gas, or mineral rights. Generally, royalty income is not considered to be a form of self-employment income and is not subject to self-employment tax. However, as with investment income and rental income, if the activity that a taxpayer engaged in that generated royalty income constitutes a trade or business for the taxpayer, the income from that activity should probably be characterized as self-employment income. There is some support, for example, for the proposition that royalties received by an author for his or her first book should not be regarded as self-employment income, whereas royalties from subsequent books should be considered self-employment income, since the taxpayer's continuing efforts, as an author, would indicate that the he or she had taken up writing as a trade or business.

Deducting Business Losses

Taxpayers are entitled to fully use losses that they suffer as a result of self-employment business activity to offset any other income that they have for the year. However, taxpayers are not entitled to deduct their net losses that were from hobbies, rather than from bona fide business activities. Many people who engage in expensive hobbies—such as accumulating collectible items, raising and maintaining pets, or owning boats, aircraft, or vintage cars—attempt to take write-offs for expenses associated with these activities in order to subsidize their hobbies with tax savings. Therefore, Congress passed specific legislation that limits the deductibility of expenses associated with a hobby to those that are deductible regardless of whether a hobby was somehow involved, such as allowing a deduction for home mortgage interest even though part of the home may have been used in connection with the taxpayer's hobby. Taxpayers are allowed to deduct the expenses incurred from a hobby to the extent that the hobby generated income.

EXAMPLE:
Rick bought a hot air balloon that he used for his own amusement on weekends. A merchant agreed to pay $200 a month to Rick if he would attach a banner to the balloon advertising his store. Rick's cost to fuel his burner and cover the maintenance and insurance on the balloon was $5,000 for the year. Rick will be permitted to use $2,400 of his annual expenses as a deduction on his Schedule A of Form 1040 to offset the $2,400 payment that he received from the merchant, but since ballooning is a hobby for Rick, he will not be permitted to use the remaining $2,600 in expenses to generate a deductible loss. If Rick were to have

received $6,500 for displaying the merchant's banner, he could use his full $5,000 in expenses as a deduction on his Schedule A of Form 1040 to offset $5,000 of his receipts, but would have to report the remaining $1,500 as taxable income, even though it was from a hobby, despite the fact that he cannot take a write-off for any net losses from the hobby.

It should be readily apparent that, in many cases, it would be far preferable for a taxpayer's activities to be considered to have been engaged in for a profit, rather than a hobby. Since conflicts often arise between taxpayers and IRS auditors over this issue, Congress has attempted to resolve the matter to some degree by including a safe-harbor presumption in I.R.C. §183(d). If the gross income from an activity exceeds the deductions attributable to it for three or more of the taxable years of the five consecutive taxable years ending with the year in question, §183(d) provides that it shall be presumed that the activity was engaged in for a profit. Special provisions are made for those engaged in the breeding, training, showing, or racing of horses, in which case §183(d) provides for the presumption that the activity was engaged in for a profit if a profit was made in two or more of the taxable years of the seven consecutive taxable years ending with the year in question.

When it is presumed that an activity is engaged in for profit under the provisions of I.R.C. §183(d), that presumption applies to all of the years for the five-year or seven-year period involved. At the inception of an activity, it may be

TIP—

You are entitled to fully use losses that you suffer as a result of self-employment business activity to offset any other income that you have for the year.

presumed by a party that the activity will generate income in excess of expenses for at least three of the first five years of the activity, resulting in the taxpayer using losses in the first year or two of the activity to offset other income. However, if the taxpayer ultimately fails to realize the anticipated profits from the activity, he or she will not meet the criteria of §183(d) necessary to be presumed to be engaged in an activity for profit, as was also anticipated. Normally, I.R.C. §6501 requires that the IRS assess any tax to be imposed on a taxpayer within three years of the later of the due date for which a timely return was filed, or the actual filing date for a return that was filed late, provided that the return was not a fraudulent return or one that omitted more than 25% of the taxpayer's properly includible gross income. However, §183(e)(4) extends the time for the IRS to make assessments to two years after the due date of the return for the last year in the five-year or seven-year period relevant for making the presumption as to whether an activity of a taxpayer was engaged in for profit, when the taxpayer had income or losses from activities that bring that issue into question.

Combining Activities in Order to Qualify for the Presumption

A common device used by taxpayers in order to avoid having an activity that generates losses from being categorized as a hobby, and losing the opportunity to use those losses to offset other income, is to lump those activities together with other activities that generate sufficient profit to more than offset the losses, thus treating the combined activities as a single activity. Treasury Regulation §1.183-1(d)(1) states that, "generally, the Commissioner will accept the characterization by the taxpayer of several undertakings either as a single activity or as separate activities. The taxpayer's characterization will not be accepted, however, when it appears that this characterization is artificial and cannot reasonably be supported under the facts and circumstances of the case." In making the determination of whether a taxpayer has properly combined several activities into a single activity for purposes of determining whether or not the activity should be regarded as having been engaged in for a profit, Regulation §1.183-1(d)(1) requires that all the facts and circumstances of the case must be taken into account, and states that the most significant among them are:

- the degree of organizational and economic relationship of various undertakings;
- the business purpose, which is (or might be) served by carrying on the various undertakings separately or together in a trade or business or in an investment setting; and,
- the similarity of various undertakings.

Application of these factors will almost always leave sufficient room for disagreement to attract the attention of an IRS auditor in cases in which they are relevant.

TIP—

Application of the most significant factors in determining whether a taxpayer has properly combined several activities into a single activity for determining whether the activity was engaged in for a profit will almost always leave sufficient room for disagreement to attract the attention of an IRS auditor.

Proving a Profit Motive When the Presumption Does Not Apply

Taxpayers who fail to meet the *safe-harbor test*, even if they have activities to combine and are permitted to do so, can still avoid being considered to be engaged in a hobby if they can show that the activity in question was engaged in for a profit. The Treasury has issued Regulation §1.183-2 for making such a determination. It requires that the taxpayer entered into or continued an activity with the objective of making a profit, even though it may not have been reasonable to expect to make a profit. In fact, the Regulation states that "it may be sufficient that there is a small chance of making a large profit in determining" that an activity has been engaged in for the purpose of making a profit. The Regulation specifically cites an investment in a wildcat oil well, which requires a substantial investment despite a low probability of success, as an example of a venture considered to be engaged in for profit, although it is unlikely, perhaps even to the point of being an unreasonable expectation, that profit from the venture will ever be realized.

There are a number of factors set forth in Regulation §§1.183-2(b)(1) through (9) for use in determining whether a taxpayer engaged in an activity for the purpose of making a profit. However, the Regulation acknowledges that the list is not exhaustive, and specifically provides in §1.183(b) that factors other than those listed may be considered in making the determination. Most of the nine factors set forth in the Regulation are somewhat subjective. Among the most highly subjective of the group are the manner in which the taxpayer carries on the activity; the expertise of the taxpayer or his or her advisors; the expectation that assets used in the activity may appreciate; the success of the taxpayer in carrying on other activities; and, the elements of personal pleasure or recreation that the taxpayer gets from the activity.

Tip—

Among the most highly subjective of the factors used to determine whether a taxpayer engaged in an activity for the purpose of making a profit include:
- the manner in which the taxpayer carries on the activity;
- the expertise of the taxpayer or his or her advisors;
- the expectation that assets used in the activity may appreciate;
- the success of the taxpayer in carrying on other activities; and,
- the elements of personal pleasure or recreation that the taxpayer gets from the activity.

Since the primary purpose of the IRS categorizing a taxpayer's activity as a hobby (rather than a venture for profit) is to prevent the losses from the activity from being used to offset income from such sources as wages or salary from a job, when a taxpayer shows losses from an activity for enough years that it will not qualify for the presumption that he or she is engaged in an activity for a profit, there is considerable likelihood that the IRS will single the taxpayer out for an audit. The IRS auditor will then prevail upon the taxpayer to convincingly apply the nine factors set forth in the Regulation and establish a profit motive. This is a particularly attractive situation for the IRS to audit, since a finding that an activity was a hobby—rather than one engaged in for profit—will result in disallowance of write-offs for those losses for several years, and there is the potential to recover a very large tax deficiency along with penalty and interest as well.

TIP—

If the IRS can reclassify your activity as a hobby from one engaged in for a profit, it is a particularly attractive situation for the IRS, since such a finding will result in disallowance of write-offs for those losses for several years, and there is the potential to recover a very large tax deficiency along with penalty and interest.

Taking a Deduction For An In-Home Office

Self-employed taxpayers commonly operate their businesses from their homes to at least some degree. As a result, they then believe that they can justify taking a business deduction for that part of their home that was put to business use. Since such taxpayers do not actually make a payment for a home office, as they would were they to rent commercial office space, determining the value and appropriateness of a deduction for a home office is somewhat subjective, and has been the object of abuse by taxpayers through the years. As a result, Congress has set forth some rather stringent requirements in I.R.C. §280A, which taxpayers must meet in order to qualify for a home office deduction.

Uses That Must Be Both Exclusive and Regular

As long as part of a taxpayer's residence is used exclusively and regularly for business, §280A(C)(1) permits a deduction if the use is:
- as the principal place of business for any trade or business of the taxpayer;
- as a place of business used by patients, clients, or customers in meeting or dealing with the taxpayer in the normal course of his or her trade or business; or,
- a separate structure not attached to the dwelling unit that is used in connection with the taxpayer's trade or business.

The requirement that a party must use some portion of his or her residence exclusively for business use in order to qualify for a deduction is a strict one. When exclusive business use is required, there is no tolerance and even minimal nonbusiness use will disqualify the expense for a deduction.

EXAMPLE:
Jean, a self-employed typist, set up her living room as her office, and usually kept the room covered with books and papers. On major holidays and a few other occasions during the year, Jean would clean out the room and use it to entertain her family and guests during parties. Even though these nonbusiness uses of

her living room were very limited, they would disqualify her from taking a business deduction in connection with its business use.

It is not necessary to devote a separate room of a residence to business use as long as there is a definite area devoted to regular, exclusive business use. Congregating business-related furnishings and equipment into a single area rather than scattering them throughout various parts of the residence would likely be essential in establishing exclusive business use of a definite part of a residence.

Section 280A offers no guidance as to what constitutes regular use of a space for business purposes. Therefore, the term *regular* should be given its ordinary meaning, which would require a steady, ongoing, and frequent use, as opposed to a sporadic or occasional use, even if the total hours of sporadic use exceeded the total hours of ongoing use. Even if a self-employed person has his or her principal place of business at a fixed site away from home, §280A still allows a deduction for that part of his or her home that a taxpayer regularly uses exclusively to meet or deal with patients, clients, or customers.

The third general deduction provision in §280A applies to business use of structures located on the premises of a taxpayer's residence but that are not attached to the dwelling. Such free-standing structures as a studio would qualify for the deduction, but the entire structure, rather than a mere part of it, must be used exclusively and regularly for the taxpayer's trade or business. However, §280A does not require that a separate structure located on the site of a taxpayer's residence be the primary place that a party

TIP—

The requirement that a party must use some portion of his or her residence exclusively for business use in order to qualify for a deduction is a strict one, with even minimal nonbusiness use disqualifying the deduction.

conducts a trade or business, nor does it require the party to meet patients, clients, or customers there in order to take a deduction for it, as long as it is used exclusively and regularly in his or her trade or business.

Uses That Must Be Regular But Not Exclusive

A taxpayer who is in the business of providing day care for children, persons who are at least 65 years of age, or individuals who are incapable of caring for themselves due to mental or physical incapacity, and who regularly uses some part of his or her residence to provide those services, is allowed by §280A to take a deduction for the part of the residence used for that business. It is not necessary that the part of the residence used for a day care be exclusively used for that purpose, as long as the space is available for regular use in providing day care services and is used for that purpose more than merely occasionally. However, a deduction for use of part of one's residence as a day care will be denied if the taxpayer has failed to obtain authority to do so under state law, such as a license to operate such a facility.

The other deduction provided for in §280A that requires regular use of part of a residence for business purposes, but does not require exclusive use, is the one for allocation of space within one's residence for the purpose of storing inventory or product samples in connection with the party's trade or business of selling products at either the retail or wholesale level. Although the area used for storage does not have to be exclusively used for that purpose in order for the taxpayer to be eligible for the deduction, §280A does require that the party's residence be the sole fixed location of such trade or business in order to qualify for the deduction.

What Draws Attention From the IRS Toward Home Offices

Because of the rather precise requirements that taxpayers must meet in order to qualify for a home office deduction, auditors are often able to successfully challenge taxpayers' eligibility to take the deduction. A visit to a taxpayer's home office by an auditor may clearly show that the taxpayer has failed to meet one or more of the requirements. Even taxpayers who qualify for a home office deduction are subject to being challenged on the issue of the size of their deductions, since they may have allocated more of their home to office space than actually qualifies or may have miscalculated the amount of such a deduction that they were qualified to take.

Engaging In Bartering

Exchanging goods or services for other goods or services, rather than selling them for money, is a practice known as *bartering*. It is not illegal to engage in bartering, but taxpayers who do so are required to report the fair market value of the goods and services that they barter for as part of their receipts when they calculate their taxable incomes. Since the goods and services received from bartering will not be deposited in a bank account and are rarely tracked by W-2 forms or 1099 forms, they are difficult to detect. As a result, bartering has become a popular way to do business among tax protesters and others looking for a way to evade their obligation to pay taxes without being caught. This is why engaging in bartering will likely cause a taxpayer to be selected for an IRS audit.

Some people get so involved in bartering that they join bartering clubs whose membership rolls can provide the IRS with a list of audit candidates in the event that the

TIP—

Bartering is difficult to detect and has become a popular way to do business among tax protesters and others looking for a way to evade their obligation to pay taxes without being caught. This is why engaging in bartering will likely cause a taxpayer to be selected for an IRS audit.

barter club is audited. Also, if someone who has been involved in bartering is audited and that party reveals the identity of his or her bartering partners, the IRS will probably target those parties next.

One of the first questions that auditors usually ask taxpayers who are being audited is whether they belong to a barter club or have otherwise engaged in bartering. If the taxpayer admits to such activity, the auditor will then want the details of the taxpayer's bartering. If a taxpayer who has engaged in bartering or belongs to a barter club states that he or she is not a member of a barter club and has not engaged in bartering, he or she runs the risk of being set up by the auditor, who has already learned of the taxpayer's activities from the audit of the barter club that the party belongs to or an audit of a bartering partner. Knowingly making false statements to an IRS auditor is a criminal offense that is punishable by up to five years in prison or a $10,000 fine, or both.

Taking Abnormally Large Itemized Deductions

Even taxpayers who are not self-employed and are therefore ineligible to take business deductions may still qualify to take a deduction for itemized personal deductions on Schedule A of Form 1040. Taxpayers are permitted to take a standard deduction based on their filing status, but those whose itemized deductions exceed their standard deduction will benefit from taking the itemized deductions. As with business deductions, the IRS has collected historical data from taxpayers' returns and used it to develop norms for the various types of deductible expenditures for various groups of taxpayers, broken down by such factors as age, family size, and geographic location of residence. Additionally, the IRS has developed some audit guidelines for the general population based on the relative size of taxpayers' itemized deductions.

Taxpayers whose itemized deductions on Schedule A are less than 35% of their adjusted gross income will fall well within the norm and are not likely to be subjected to an audit on the basis of those deductions. On the other hand, if such deductions are 45% or more of a taxpayer's adjusted gross income, there is a significant increase in the likelihood of an audit being triggered due to the size of those deductions. In the range in which itemized deductions exceed 35% but are not as high as 45%, the likelihood of audit due to abnormally high itemized deductions transitions from little likelihood to relatively high likelihood.

TIP—

If your itemized deductions are less than 35% of your adjusted gross income, you are not likely to be subjected to an audit on the basis of those deductions. If your itemized deductions exceed 35% but are less than 45%, the likelihood of an audit increases. If your itemized deductions exceed 45%, there is a significant increase in the likelihood of an audit being triggered due to the size of those deductions.

Other Activities That May Trigger An Audit

There are several specific categories of taxpayers who are more likely to become targets of IRS audits than others. Tax returns filed by those whose incomes exceed $100,000 have traditionally been more likely to be audited than those of lower income earners. With limited resources and manpower, it is simply more cost-effective for the IRS to audit the returns of those whose mistakes are most likely to result in relatively significant tax deficiencies. However, the IRS frequently changes its targeted groups, and in recent years, lower income earners have been getting a larger percentage of letters from the IRS informing them that, due to some omission or clerical error, they owe more taxes than reflected on the tax returns that they filed.

Past audits that resulted in a tax deficiency will make future audits more likely. Future audits in such situations are easy to justify, since one or more past audits revealed a propensity on the taxpayer's part to file inaccurate returns. Also, past success in collecting additional taxes from a taxpayer is likely to foster the belief that devoting some of the resources available to the IRS to a subsequent audit of that same taxpayer will be more efficient than auditing someone who has not been audited before and has no proven history of filing inaccurate returns.

Taxpayers who claim losses from tax shelters are also more likely to be audited than those who do not. *Tax shelters* are generally investment schemes that generate losses for accounting purposes, but often do not involve actual monetary losses. Historically, many of these types of investments have not met the criteria set forth in the Internal Revenue Code to permit a deduction for losses generated by them. Therefore, losses from tax shelters almost automatically raise questions of legitimacy in the minds of IRS auditors.

The likelihood of an audit is also increased when a taxpayer's tax return includes alimony payments or casualty losses, and when he or she claims someone as a dependent who does not live with him or

TIP—

Other groups or circumstances that may trigger an audit include:
- taxpayers whose income exceed $100,000;
- taxpayers whose past audits resulted in a tax deficiency;
- taxpayers who claim losses from tax shelters; and,
- taxpayers whose tax returns include alimony payments or casualty losses, or claim someone as a dependent who does not live with him or her.

her (such as a parent), and claims an exemption deduction for that person. The rules for taking these tax write-offs are fairly stringent and complex, and upon close scrutiny, taxpayers are often found to fail to qualify for them.

Taxpayers whose circumstances cause them to legitimately fall into one of the groups that is at greater risk of audit may not be able to do much to change that. Certainly, taxpayers should claim every legitimate deduction to which they are entitled. However, taxpayers who are aware that entering certain professions or claiming certain deductions will put them under closer scrutiny should pay careful attention to meeting the criteria that must be met to entitle them to favorable tax treatment, and should be especially meticulous in their recordkeeping.

SECTION III

RESPONDING TO AUDIT NOTICES AND DEALING WITH DEFICIENCIES

Taxpayers who have received audit notices from the IRS have some latitude in how they may respond. There is no doubt that the way in which they respond will have a significant affect on the outcome of the audit. Furthermore, taxpayers also have some choices in how they respond to an auditor's findings. There are also a variety of ways for taxpayers to deal with taxes that have been assessed, regardless of whether those taxes were assessed due to the findings of an auditor or otherwise. This section addresses these matters, providing strong guidance in how to respond to an audit notice and how to deal with any deficiencies.

Chapter Eight

Preparing For an Audit and Responding to the Findings

Although the formal audit process will not begin until a taxpayer receives a notice from the IRS that he or she has been selected for an audit, preparation for an audit should begin at the very beginning of the party's tax year. The first step in that preparation process is the establishment of an efficient procedure for keeping the necessary records to accurately establish income and deductible expenses. Taxpayers who intend to claim someone as a dependent under circumstances that may be questionable, such as when the dependent does not reside with them, should also keep accurate records of expenses that are not deductible, but that relate to them providing support.

Keeping Proper Records

The specific types of records that a taxpayer should maintain will depend on the particular party's situation. It is imperative for self-employed taxpayers to keep accurate records of their business receipts as well as their deductible business expenses. Not only are such records essential in the event that a taxpayer is audited and must provide supporting documentation for the figures shown on his or her return, but keeping accurate records will prevent a self-employed person from inadvertently including nonbusiness receipts. If, through poor recordkeeping or other mistake, a self-employed person includes nonbusiness receipts—such as wages earned from a job as someone else's employee or interest income from savings—in with his or her self-employment income, he or she will be overstating self-employment earnings, and thus paying more in taxes. Accurate records will also help ensure that self-employed taxpayers do not overstate their self-employment earnings by failing to take all of their business deductions to the full extent that they are entitled to take them.

One of the best ways for self-employed taxpayers to keep their business-related income and expenses separate from their nonbusiness income and personal expenses is to open a separate checking account for their business activity. Otherwise, if they commingle their business and nonbusiness deposits and expenditures in a single account, they will have to sort them out at some later time, and there is a significant chance of errors during the sorting process. Although cancelled checks provide proof of expenditures, taxpayers should also retain receipts that detail the nature of the purchases that they have made, since an auditor may demand proof not only that a claimed expense was actually incurred, but also proof as to what was actually acquired with the expenditure.

Many credit card companies now offer very detailed billing that allows customers to code in expenditures so that their bill will indicate which charges are for expenditures that the cardholder believes are deductible. Retaining receipts will be necessary to support deductions based on

> **TIP—**
>
> Accurate records will help ensure that self-employed taxpayers do not overstate their self-employment earnings by failing to take all of the business deductions that they are entitled to take.

those charges, since the credit card bill will show the identity of the merchant who was paid, but may not give sufficient details of the transaction to support the validity of taking a deduction for the expenditure.

Auto Expense Records

Among the most important records that self-employed taxpayers should keep are log books that show the number of miles that they drive in connection with their self-employment activities. Taxpayers who use a vehicle entirely for business will not be required to keep a log, since 100% of their mileage is for business. However, taxpayers who use their vehicles partly for business must keep a mileage log, or they run the risk of having their deductions for the business use of their vehicles disallowed.

Taxpayers who take a business deduction for automobile expenses must indicate on their returns whether the vehicle is used only partly for business, and if so, whether they have a written record of their business use, as well as their personal and commuting use. No deduction is generally allowed for auto expenses associated with commuting and personal use. Taxpayers who indicate that they do not have a written record to support their auto expense deduction may simply receive correspondence to the effect that their auto expense deduction has been disallowed, or it may be a factor that results in their being selected for an audit.

Mileage records kept to support an auto expense deduction should be kept on a daily basis so that they are what are known as *contemporaneous records*, rather than being reconstructed at the end of the taxpayer's tax year. However, auditors do sometimes allow taxpayers to reconstruct mileage records when they have failed to keep them contemporaneously.

TIP—

If you indicate that you do not have a written record to support your auto expense deduction, you may find yourself selected for an audit.

EXAMPLE:

Parthenia has a part-time job as a newspaper carrier in order to supplement her income as a foot model for a shoe store chain. The IRS chose to audit her return, and during the course of the audit, she admitted that she had failed to keep a log book of her business mileage. Since Parthenia covered the same route every day and worked seven days a week without missing a day, she would likely be permitted to clock her miles driven on her route for one day and multiply that total by 365 to arrive at a year's business mileage total.

Taxpayers whose business use of their automobiles is erratic are likely to have a much harder time convincing an IRS auditor to allow them to reconstruct the records that they need to support their deduction. The only safe approach is to keep good, contemporaneous mileage records when an auto expense deduction is anticipated.

There are two different ways in which taxpayers can calculate their vehicle deduction expense. One is to multiply their number of miles by the IRS allowable rate. The other way is to take what is known as *actual expenses*, which are the expenses associated with the business use of a vehicle. Since there are two different ways, there may be some confusion as to when you should keep mileage records. If you calculate your mileage deductions by multiplying your business miles by the number of cents that the IRS allows per mile, the need to keep up with your business mileage is readily apparent. On the other hand, if you are basing your auto expense deduction on the actual expenses associated with the use of your vehicle, you may think that you do not need to keep up with your business mileage. However, if you use a vehicle for both business and nonbusiness driving, you will be required to allocate those expenses between your business and nonbusiness driving on the basis of the miles driven for each purpose. Therefore, keeping up with business and nonbusiness mileage is just as important for taxpayers who use their vehicles only partly for business and base their deduction on their actual expenses as it is for those who use their vehicles only partly for business and base their deductions on the allowable cents-per-mile rate.

Records of Business Meals and Entertainment

In light of the fact that taxpayers who take business deductions for meals and entertainment expenses are often targeted for an audit and the requirements to qualify for deduction of those expenses are somewhat stringent, it is imperative that taxpayers who anticipate such deductions keep proper records to support those deductions. Merely maintaining cancelled checks, credit card receipts, and cash receipts— even when accompanied by a merchant's detailed receipt describing the meal or entertainment that was purchased—is not enough. Such proof establishes that those purchases were made, but does not support the taxpayer's contention that they were provided to clients or others under circumstances that would make their cost deductible. Certainly, it is necessary to maintain proof that expenditures for claimed deductions for business meals and entertainment were actually made, but it is also necessary to supplement those records with details concerning the identity of the parties who were present, the purpose of the business meeting, the nature of the business that was discussed, and the setting in which the business discussions took place.

At a minimum, taxpayers should make notes of such information on the backs of the receipts that they get for expenditures for business meals and entertainment. Ideally, taxpayers with deductible expenditures for business meals

TIP—

Taxpayers who take business deductions for meals and entertainment expenses are often targeted for audit.

TIP—

The necessary recordkeeping for meal and entertainment deductions includes:

- proof that expenditures for claimed deductions for business meals and entertainment were actually made;
- details concerning the identity of the parties who were present;
- the purpose of the business meeting;
- the nature of the business that was discussed; and,
- the setting in which the business discussions took place.

and entertainment should keep a log book, which may even be incorporated in their mileage log, in which detailed information is kept that justifies the deductibility for their expenditures for business meals and entertainment.

Supporting Schedule A Deductions

Taxpayers who find it advantageous to itemize deductions on Schedule A of Form 1040, rather than take the standard deduction, will need to maintain records to support those deductions. Taxpayers who are not sure whether their itemized deductions will exceed their allowable standard deduction would be wise to maintain records of their deductible expenses from the beginning of the year, rather than having to try and reconstruct those records at the end of the year. Reconstructing records can be so tedious that taxpayers who have sufficient deductible expenses that itemizing would benefit them may opt to take the standard deduction rather than go through the process of assembling records of their expenditures.

Fortunately for most taxpayers, other parties have taken on many of their recordkeeping responsibilities for them. Charitable organizations keep records of their donors' cash contributions and report them to the parties in total at the end of the year, leaving taxpayers with the duty of maintaining records of only their noncash contributions among their charitable donations. Also, mortgage companies and other lenders supply their customers with annual reports concerning the amount of mortgage interest that they have paid, as well as the amount of any property taxes paid by the lender on behalf of the borrower.

On the other hand, taxpayers will be fully responsible for their own recordkeeping for some of the expenditures that qualify for a personal deduction. For instance, taxpayers who qualify for a deduction for medical expenses will need to maintain records of the medical insurance premiums that they pay, their uninsured medical and dental expenses, and even their travel expenses to and from medical providers.

Among the less stringent recordkeeping requirements for taxpayers who itemize personal deductions are payments of property taxes made directly by them and payments of state income taxes, since the information is readily available from the entity that collected it or from state tax returns that were filed. Also, mortgage interest paid to individuals who carry owner financing and are not required to report it can be readily ascertained from an amortization schedule.

Among the more difficult documentation tasks for individuals is the chore of determining value of property that has been damaged or destroyed, and for which the taxpayer intends to take a deduction for a casualty loss on Schedule A. Goods that are stolen or completely destroyed will not be available for an appraiser to evaluate, and even partially destroyed property may be difficult to evaluate. That is why it is advisable to take pictures of household furnishings and collectibles, and perhaps get appraisals of

TIP—

Reconstructing records can be so tedious that taxpayers who have sufficient deductible expenses that itemizing would benefit them may opt to take the standard deduction rather than go through the process of assembling records of their expenditures.

jewelry, antiques, and collectibles before they suffer any damage and keep that documentation in a separate place, such as a safe-deposit box, so that the same peril that destroys an owner's property will not also destroy the documentation as to that property's value.

The most stringent recordkeeping requirement falls on taxpayers who take an itemized deduction for unreimbursed employee expenses on Schedule A. Among those who most commonly fit into this category are outside sales people who are employees, but whose employers do not cover their cost of travel, meals and entertainment, purchase of samples, and other costs associated with their jobs. Although they are not self-employed, in order to support their deductions for these expenses, they will need to keep the same types of records, such as mileage logs and details concerning business meals and entertainment, that self-employed taxpayers are required to keep.

TIP—

Taxpayers who take an itemized deduction for unreimbursed employee expenses need to keep the same types of records, such as mileage logs and details concerning business meals and entertainment, that self-employed taxpayers are required to keep.

Making Notes During Preparation of Tax Returns

Generally, by the time a taxpayer receives notice of having been selected for an audit, it has been years since the return in question was prepared. As a result, it is not uncommon for taxpayers to have little recollection of the details of the return. Therefore, it is essential for taxpayers to make detailed notes concerning how they arrived at their reported income and the deductions, exemptions, and credits that they took when it is not obvious. For example, a party who takes a business deduction for a home office should make notes on how the percentage of the home that was dedicated to office use was determined and the mathematical calculations of the deduction that was taken. Sometimes a brief explanation written beside an entry on the taxpayer's copy of the return may be sufficient. These notes are not to be sent to the IRS. Only the basic required return should be sent, since added notes may draw unwanted attention to the return. The purpose of the notes is to refresh the taxpayer's memory in the event that he or she has to explain items on his or her tax return at a time when the party may not otherwise remember much about it. Taxpayers who use paid preparers should either review their returns with the preparers and make notes, or insist that the preparers make such notes as they prepare the returns.

Responding to an Audit Notice

Once a taxpayer receives an official notice from the IRS informing him or her that his or her return has been selected for an audit, he or she should contact a qualified party to represent him or her for the audit. Qualified parties include CPAs, attorneys, enrolled agents, and preparers of the taxpayer's return. If the taxpayer's return was prepared by a preparer who is not an attorney or CPA, or is otherwise not well-qualified to represent him or her at an IRS audit, it would probably be best to engage the services of a more qualified party than the preparer.

In order to be represented by someone during an audit, the taxpayer must execute a Form 2848, Power of Attorney,

TIP—

If you are selected for an audit and your return was prepared by a preparer who is not an attorney or CPA, or is otherwise not well-qualified to represent you at an IRS audit, it would probably be best to engage the services of a more qualified party than the preparer.

appointing the party of his or her choice as his or her agent for the audit. The form must specify the type of audit, such as an audit of Form 1040, and year or years for which the appointment is made.

When taxpayers appoint agents to represent them in an IRS audit, they usually never have to appear. Other than perhaps calling the IRS to reschedule an appointment in order to have more time to choose a representative to send in their place, taxpayers should not deal directly with an IRS auditor without being represented. Taxpayers should definitely not even attend the initial meeting with an IRS auditor. Some people, in an effort to avoid having to pay a professional representative's fee, go to the first meeting with auditors, intending to get a feel for whether or not they need representation. This is a bad idea. If a taxpayer who attended an initial meeting with the IRS auditor without representation were to later decide to hire a representative, the individual may have already made statements that will be difficult to overcome, and the representative will not even know what was actually said at that meeting.

A cardinal rule for any taxpayer dealing with an IRS auditor is to never lie to the auditor. If a taxpayer were to fear that an answer to an auditor's question might prove to be incriminating, he or she should refuse to answer it, rather than give a false answer. Some taxpayers attempt to lie their way out of incriminating situations that are brought up by IRS auditors. However, since making false statements to IRS agents is a crime that is punishable by up to five years in prison, a $10,000 fine, or both, that would be an ill-advised strategy. By having an opportunity to have an IRS auditor's questions filtered through a representative who is a tax professional, who will later respond with the answer to the auditor, taxpayers will be able to provide more considered answers, will be advised not to answer when that is the prudent course of action, and will not be tempted to give false answers.

TIP—

A cardinal rule for any taxpayer dealing with an IRS auditor is to never lie to the auditor.

Chapter Nine

Responding to Audit Results and Tax Deficiencies

Internal Revenue Service audits can actually result in a refund to the party being audited if a taxpayer made mistakes on a return that resulted in a larger tax liability than was actually owed. Some audits simply confirm that the return was properly filled out as it was filed and there is no change in the taxpayer's tax liability. Still others result in a determination that the return that was filed by the taxpayer contained errors that, when corrected, will result in a tax deficiency. The taxpayer will then be assessed for the tax deficiency, plus interest, and may be assessed for penalties, as well. There are penalties for negligent preparation of one's tax return, and more severe penalties for willful noncompliance with the tax laws. The imposition of penalties is an issue that can be negotiated with auditors, but the imposition of interest is not.

Auditors are not supposed to split tax issues, such as allowing a taxpayer to take half of a questionable deduction as a compromise. However, if a taxpayer could offer proof of expenditures for only half of a clearly deductible item that was claimed, it would certainly be appropriate for an auditor to allow the half that was substantiated and disallow the half that was not.

If a taxpayer is dissatisfied with the results of an audit, the party may request an opportunity to meet with the auditor's supervisor in an effort to resolve disagreements. Once a party has been given a copy of the IRS auditor's report, the taxpayer has thirty days to appeal the auditor's findings to the Appeals Division, which is an office attached to the Department of Justice. The Appeals Division does have authority to split tax issues in an effort to reach a settlement, and it settles the vast majority of cases it receives. Action beyond this point will require litigation by the taxpayer.

If auditors conclude that a taxpayer is guilty of fraud or other tax crimes, they may elect to refer the case to the Criminal Investigation Division of the IRS. Agents within that division, known as *special agents*, have the authority to subpoena books and records of the taxpayer and of third parties, and can even obtain search warrants to aid in their investigation as they compile evidence against the suspected violator. Once their investigation is complete, if they believe that the evidence warrants prosecution, the Criminal Investigation Division of the IRS must then present that evidence to the Department of Justice, which will have sole discretion as to whether or not to prosecute.

Dealing with a Tax Deficiency

If you are required to file a tax return, you should do so whether or not you can actually pay your taxes. Failure to file a timely tax return that is required will result in interest and penalties on any tax deficiencies, and could even lead to criminal prosecution. If a party files a timely, accurate return without paying any resulting tax liability, the IRS can impose

TIP—

If you file a timely, accurate return without paying any resulting tax liability, the IRS can impose interest on the unpaid tax liability, but you will not be guilty of a crime.

interest on the unpaid tax liability, but the taxpayer will not be guilty of a crime. In the event that a taxpayer is unable to pay a tax liability, regardless of whether the liability arose due to inability to pay the tax liability with the return that showed the liability or the liability resulted from an additional assessment following an audit, there are several options available to deal with the deficiency.

Consequences of Failure to Pay Taxes

Taxpayers who do not actively deal with the IRS to resolve their tax deficiencies may have to face some harsh consequences. To start with, the IRS can use the authority granted to it in I.R.C. §6321 to file a tax lien against the taxpayer. The tax lien gives notice to the taxpayer that he or she is no longer free to sell or convey property that he or she owns. No one who is aware of such a lien would want to buy the property, since it would be acquired subject to the lien. Also, creditors will not generally lend money to taxpayers with tax liens, because they fear that any collateral acquired by the parties may be caught up in the lien or that future collection efforts will adversely affect the taxpayers' ability to repay the loan. Since the IRS files tax liens in the public records where the parties live and where they own real estate, everyone is deemed to be aware of the lien, whether they actually are or not. Therefore, lenders and those considering buying realty or significant amounts of personal property from someone will search the public records for such liens.

The IRS also has the right to seize and sell a delinquent taxpayer's property under the levy and distraint provisions of I.R.C. §6331. All that is required is that the taxpayer be given at least thirty days' written notice of the service's intent to levy. The notice may be delivered in person, left at the party's home or business, or sent by certified or registered mail. If it appears that waiting thirty days before executing the levy would place collection of taxes in jeopardy, such as when it seems likely that the party might flee the country with assets, the IRS is permitted to levy a taxpayer's property without giving notice.

Section 6334 of the I.R.C. exempts a few things from levy, such as necessary clothing, school books, up to $6,250 worth of household furnishings and effects, up to $3,125 worth of tools of a trade or profession, unemployment benefits, some pension payments, workers' compensation benefits, and a base amount of wages. Otherwise, a taxpayer's wages, salaries, and other income, both accrued and anticipated, can be levied, and a sizable amount of it seized by the IRS. Even a taxpayer's principal residence is subject to levy by the IRS to pay delinquent taxes.

Although it is not a crime to be unable to pay a tax deficiency, concealing assets from the IRS so that they cannot levy them constitutes payment evasion, which is a crime under I.R.C. §7201 and carries a penalty of up to five years' imprisonment, a fine of up to $100,000 ($500,000 for corporations), or both, plus the costs of prosecution. The IRS locates the assets of a delinquent taxpayer by asking him or her to complete a Form 433A for individuals or Form 433B for businesses. These require the party to list every asset he or she owns, identify banks and account numbers where he or she has deposits, and otherwise list the whereabouts of his or her property. If the taxpayer refuses to fill out the appropriate Form 433, the IRS may summon the

TIP—

Items exempt from an IRS tax levy include:

- necessary clothing;
- school books;
- up to $6,250 worth of household furnishings and effects;
- up to $3,125 worth of tools of a trade or profession;
- unemployment benefits;
- some pension payments;
- workers' compensation benefits; and,
- a base amount of wages.

taxpayer and require the party to supply the same information as that requested on the Form 433 under oath. Providing false information on a Form 433 or upon oral examination would constitute perjury as well as payment evasion.

Installment Agreements

A taxpayer who cannot pay a tax deficiency in a lump sum, but who has property that is in jeopardy of being seized by the IRS to satisfy an obligation, can deal with the deficiency by making arrangements to pay it on installment. The IRS is authorized to enter into such arrangements by virtue of I.R.C. §6159. Taxpayers may initiate their requests to enter into installment arrangements by filing a Form 9465 requesting such an arrangement and proposing terms of payment. Taxpayers who can demonstrate to the IRS that they cannot pay their tax delinquency in full and agree to fully pay it within three years cannot be refused a request for an installment agreement if the delinquency does not exceed $10,000, they filed their returns on time for the past five years, and they paid any tax liability for those years without having to enter into an installment agreement in order to do so. A taxpayer whose tax delinquency does not exceed $10,000 is not required to submit a Form 433 listing the party's assets when the request is submitted for an installment agreement, but the IRS may subsequently ask for one.

Taxpayers with deficiencies in excess of $10,000 are not guaranteed that they will be allowed to pay their delinquent taxes by installment. These taxpayers must convince the IRS that they are viable candidates for retiring their delinquencies on an installment basis. Those with deficiencies in excess of $10,000 must initiate their request to pay what they owe in installments by submitting the same Form 9465 that those with smaller deficiencies must submit, but an accompanying Form 433 is mandatory.

There are several criteria that a taxpayer must meet in connection with an installment agreement, and these are explained in the instructions of Form 9465. For one thing, regardless of the amount of a party's tax delinquency, the taxpayer is expected to pay as much of it as possible, borrow as much of the remaining balance as possible, and then use the installment agreement to pay only the remaining balance. Once a delinquent taxpayer is approved for an installment agreement, it is imperative that payments of the agreed-upon installments are made on time. Also, those who enter into installment agreements must comply with all of the laws concerning filing returns and the payment of taxes every year throughout the course of the agreement. If a taxpayer who has entered into an installment agreement fails to abide by any of the terms of the agreement, the IRS is free to resume collection efforts, such as levies on wages and bank accounts, and seizure and sale of property, which are otherwise suspended during the course of an installment agreement, as provided for in Treasury Regulation §301.6169-1. The IRS prefers that payments made by taxpayers under installment agreements be made by electronic funds transfer or by payroll deduction by the party's employer, but plans calling for payments by mail from the taxpayer may be accepted as well.

TIP—

The IRS prefers that payments made by taxpayers under installment agreements be made by electronic funds transfer or by payroll deduction by the party's employer, but plans calling for payments by mail from the taxpayer may be accepted as well.

In fact, most taxpayers who submit a Form 9465 and propose a non-direct debit installment payment plan must pay a fee of $105 along with the form, whereas those who propose a direct debit installment payment plan are required to pay a submission fee of only $52. Low-income earners, as defined by the U.S. Department of Health and

Human Services, are required to pay a submission fee of only $43 regardless of whether or not they propose a direct debit installment payment plan.

The maximum length of time that an installment agreement may last is sixty months, at which time the taxpayer's deficiency must be paid in full. This relatively short payment period can prove particularly burdensome to taxpayers with relatively large tax deficiencies, especially since interest continues to accumulate on the deficiency during the course of the installment agreement. In fact, the combination of a short maximum duration for installment agreements plus the continuing accumulation of interest will probably make it impractical for seriously delinquent taxpayers to address their tax deficiencies through an installment agreement. However, those with relatively modest tax deficiencies generally find the installment agreements to be a practical way to deal with them.

Offers in Compromise

The most talked about method of settling tax deficiencies with the IRS is the *offer in compromise*. The IRS has been given the authority to settle tax deficiencies by compromise by I.R.C. §7122. Only deficiencies arising from income from the sale of illegal drugs or from criminal cases that have already been referred to the Department of Justice for prosecution are ineligible for settlement through offers in compromise.

There are significant popular misconceptions concerning offers in compromise that have undoubtedly been fostered by advertisements by those seeking to represent delinquent taxpayers in which they claim to settle their client's tax deficiencies for mere pennies on the dollar. The offer in compromise is not a viable solution for a taxpayer with considerable assets who simply does not want to have to part with any of them in order to pay taxes or who just wants to try and negotiate for a lower tax liability than is actually owed. Treasury Regulation §301.7122-1(a) states that in order for the IRS to even have the authority to compromise a tax liability, there must be either doubt as to liability, doubt as to collectibility, or the need to compromise in order to achieve effective tax administration.

In order to fully settle a delinquent tax liability for less than full payment through an offer in compromise, a taxpayer must submit a formal proposal on IRS Form 656 along with a fee of $150. The form, along with instructions for its completion, may be obtained at an IRS office, ordered by mail by calling 800-388-0505, or found on the IRS website at **www.irs.gov.** Each of the three justifications contained in the Treasury Regulation are listed in Form 656 with a block next to it for the taxpayer to check to indicate the basis for the offer in compromise.

If doubt as to liability is the basis of a party's offer in compromise, the taxpayer must give a detailed explanation as to why the tax is not owed and include it with the Form 656. A taxpayer may rely on the Internal Revenue Code, Treasury Regulations, Revenue Procedures, Private Letter Rulings, and case law in arguing doubt as to tax liability.

Most taxpayers attempting to settle their tax deficiencies through an offer in compromise have a problem due to their lack of ability to pay, rather than due to a dispute as to the validity of the tax claim against them. In such cases, the party offering to settle a delinquency by compromise will not be expected to include any materials concerning the validity of the tax deficiency claimed by the IRS, since only the ability to pay is in question, and there is no dispute as to whether back taxes are owed, or even how much is owed. The information that must be supplied by a taxpayer seeking approval of an offer in compromise on the basis of inability to pay should be limited to only those factors concerning the ability to pay the tax deficiency, which at a minimum should include the appropriate Form 433 filed along with the Form 656. Explanations and documentation of developments that adversely affect a taxpayer's ability to earn income, such as declining health, should certainly be included in any offer in compromise as well.

An offer in compromise made on the basis that its acceptance will achieve effective tax administration is relatively unusual. A taxpayer whose assets are such that it would be difficult for the IRS to seize and sell them—because they are owned jointly with others who are not liable for the tax deficiency in question, the assets are unique to the point that they have little market appeal, or they are in rundown condition to the point that considerable effort and expense would be involved in readying the assets for sale—would seem to be a good candidate for such an offer. As with offers based on the offeror's ability to pay, offers in compromise submitted on the basis that acceptance will achieve effective tax administration must include the appropriate Form 433 along with Form 656. Failure to submit a required Form 433 along with Form 656 will result in rejection of the offer in compromise without it even being considered.

Offers in compromise submitted by taxpayers who have not filed all of their required tax returns will be rejected without consideration, as will those filed by taxpayers who are debtors in an open bankruptcy. Also, taxpayers who submit a Form 656 that is not completely and accurately filled out and signed by all of the taxpayers involved in the offer will face rejection of their offer without it being considered.

The position taken by the IRS in evaluating offers in compromise is that it can take all of a taxpayer's assets, sell them, and apply the proceeds to the party's tax delinquency, and then set out to recover any remaining balance by levying against the taxpayer's future earnings. Therefore, offers in compromise made on a basis other than doubt as to liability must offer the IRS a minimum of at

TIP—

If you have not filed all of your required tax returns or are in an open bankruptcy, any offers in compromise will be rejected without consideration.

least the realizable value of all of the offeror's assets subject to levy plus the amount that the IRS could expect to collect by attaching the taxpayer's earnings during the period remaining on the statute of limitations for collection of the party's tax delinquency. This is made clear in the instructions to Form 656. As a result, what the IRS generally expects in situations involving offers in compromise, submitted on a basis other than doubt as to liability, is that the taxpayer is going to obtain funds from a source that the IRS could not make the offeror obtain funds from in order to pay the proposed settlement. The most common source of those funds is gifts or loans from family members and friends. Form 656 requires that taxpayers reveal the source of the funds that they intend to use to pay their offer if it is accepted.

Most taxpayers probably think of the offer in compromise as involving a lump-sum payment in settlement of their tax liability at a compromised amount. In many instances that is the case. If the taxpayer can make full payment of the proposed offer within ninety days of its acceptance, it is considered to be a cash offer and that should be indicated on Form 656. For taxpayers who cannot manage a cash offer, there is the short-term preferred payment offer, which requires full payment of the agreed-upon amount within ninety-one days to twenty-four months from the time of acceptance of the offer, or the deferred payment offer, which allows a taxpayer to pay the compromised amount on installments over the time remaining on the statute of limitations for collection by the IRS.

Offers in compromise are an available means for settling virtually any type of delinquent tax liability, even those that cannot be discharged in bankruptcy. Included among the liabilities that can be settled by an offer in compromise is the obligation for the trust portion of payroll taxes that were collected but were never paid over to the U.S. Treasury, which is one of the obligations that cannot be discharged in bankruptcy.

Another major advantage of the offer in compromise is that it will discharge a delinquent party's entire tax obligation, including penalties and interest. Also, once an offer in compromise is accepted by the IRS, there will generally be no further accumulation of interest and penalties on the agreed-upon settlement amount, even if the taxpayer's plan calls for payment on installments. Especially appealing to taxpayers is the fact that Treasury Regulation §301.7122-1 requires the IRS to suspend levy and collection efforts upon mere submission of an offer in compromise, and running throughout the time that the offer is under consideration. However, the negative side of submitting an offer in compromise is that during the period in which the IRS must suspend levy and collection efforts while a taxpayer's offer is being considered, Form 656 provides that the taxpayer is also consenting to suspension of the running of all statutes of limitation that apply to audits of any tax returns or assessments and collection of any taxes covered by the offer in compromise. Another unfavorable aspect of making an offer in compromise is that in most instances, the taxpayer will have to submit a Form 433 revealing the nature, value, and location of all of his or her assets, which will help the IRS expedite its collection efforts in the event that the offer in compromise is rejected.

The acceptance rate for offers in compromise increased from 31% in 1997–1998 to 62% in more recent years, according to the Finance Tax Board of the IRS. Certainly, many of the offers were accepted only after considerable negotiation, which often led to taxpayers having to significantly increase their original offers in order to gain approval. The increased acceptance rate is undoubtedly a source of encouragement to seriously delinquent taxpayers, but it must be remembered that acceptance of an offer in

> **TIP—**
>
> The IRS must suspend levy and collection efforts upon mere submission of an offer in compromise and running throughout the time that the offer is under consideration.

compromise is only the beginning of the process leading to discharge of a tax delinquency. Form 656 requires that taxpayers whose offers in compromise have been accepted must agree that not only will they pay the compromised tax liability as agreed, but they will also timely file tax returns required by the Internal Revenue Code and pay all taxes when due for the longer of five years or the length of any deferred payments provided for in the offer in compromise. Default in any of these terms will render the compromise agreement void, and the IRS will be free to resume all collection efforts to recover the full amount of the taxpayer's original deficiency, including penalties and interest, plus additional interest from the time that the offer was originally accepted. If a party whose offer in compromise is accepted files bankruptcy prior to fully paying the agreed on amount, the IRS may file a claim based on the original amount rather than the amount agreed to by compromise.

New provisions concerning offers in compromise were included in the *Tax Increase Prevention and Reconciliation Act of 2005*. Under the provisions of the Act, taxpayers who make a cash offer in compromise must include a down payment of 20% of their proposed settlement when they submit their offers. Also, a taxpayer who proposes paying his or her offer in compromise over time must submit his or her first installment with his or her offer and continue to pay installments while the offer is under consideration. However, the Act also has a potential benefit for taxpayers in the form of a provision that if an offer in compromise is not rejected within twenty-four months (the IRS has historically taken a long time to decide whether or not to accept an offer), it will be deemed to have been accepted.

Discharging Tax Liability by Filing Bankruptcy

Taxpayers who are hopelessly delinquent on their taxes and are essentially insolvent may be able to obtain permanent relief from their tax liabilities by declaring bankruptcy. Chapter 7 of the U.S. Bankruptcy Code provides for discharge of tax liabilities that have first come due more than three years from the date of the filing of the delinquent taxpayer petition in bankruptcy. The mechanics of a Chapter 7 bankruptcy permit petitioners to exempt certain property, which varies from state to state, and then requires them to surrender the balance of the property that they own to a trustee who will liquidate it and use the proceeds to satisfy creditors' claims to the extent possible. Filing a Chapter 7 bankruptcy is not a viable option for the taxpayer who wants to prevent assets from being taken in order to satisfy a tax delinquency, unless the only property that the petitioner is concerned about keeping is eligible for exemption in the party's state. Still another requirement that must be met in order to discharge a tax liability by filing a bankruptcy is found in 11 U.S.C. §523(a) of the Bankruptcy Code, which requires that the petitioner must have filed a tax return pertaining to the taxes sought to be discharged more than two years prior to the filing of the case.

Taxpayers whose deficiencies are due to their being a responsible party for the trust portion of payroll taxes that were withheld from employees' earnings, but not paid over to the U.S.

> **TIP—**
>
> Even though you cannot discharge your tax liabilities at less than full value in a Chapter 13 bankruptcy, you may still be able to use it to ultimately resolve your tax delinquencies by reducing your nontax liabilities and using money that would have been used to pay those obligations to pay your taxes.

Treasury, cannot discharge their tax liability attributable to those payroll taxes, because discharge of liabilities arising from breach of a fiduciary duty is prohibited by 11 U.S.C. §523(a)(4) of the U.S. Bankruptcy Code. However, the degree to which delinquency in the payment of payroll taxes is attributed to the employer's share of Social Security taxes and Medicare taxes, it is still dischargeable in a Chapter 7 bankruptcy, since that tax liability is not due to breach of a fiduciary duty. Another tax liability that cannot be discharged in bankruptcy is that arising from a delinquency attributable to a year for which the taxpayer had previously filed a fraudulent return or had otherwise attempted to evade or defeat taxes.

Taxpayers who have significant assets that they would like to retain, rather than surrender for liquidation to pay claims against them, may find a Chapter 13 bankruptcy a workable alternative. The Chapter 13 bankruptcy, known as a *wage earner plan*, permits debtors to restructure their obligations in a way that they can pay them over a period of up to five years. Debtors are even permitted to liquidate many of their debts at less than full value. However, 11 U.S.C. §507(a) designates taxes as a priority claim in bankruptcy, and 11 U.S.C. §507(a)(2) requires that all priority claims must be paid in full in a Chapter 13 bankruptcy, before any non-priority claims are paid. Even though taxpayers cannot discharge their tax liabilities at less than full value in a Chapter 13 bankruptcy, they may still be able to use it to ultimately resolve their tax delinquencies by reducing their nontax liabilities and using money that would have been used to pay those obligations to pay their taxes.

Even taxpayers who do not have assets that they wish to protect from the reach of the bankruptcy court may have to choose to file a Chapter 13 bankruptcy to deal with their tax delinquencies since the *Bankruptcy Abuse Prevention and Consumer Protection Act of 2005* renders most people who make more than the median income for their state ineligible to file a Chapter 7 bankruptcy.

Glossary

A

accounts receivable. Monies owed to a party for goods or services that were provided, but were not paid for at the time they were provided.

accrual method of accounting. A system of income reporting that recognizes the right to receive it, rather than when it is actually received. Expenses are recognized when they are incurred, rather than when they are actually paid.

adjusted gross income. A taxpayer's gross income, less various deductions that are provided for by law (such as educator expenses, student loan interest, and alimony payments). The deductions are shown on the lower fourth of the front of Form 1040, and adjusted gross income is the last figure at the bottom of Form 1040.

B

basis. The value assigned to property in the hands of a taxpayer, upon which depreciation and gain or loss from sale or deemed sale are calculated. (The starting point for calculating a taxpayer's basis in his or her property is usually its original cost, plus capital improvements, less depreciation and insurance proceeds received for losses that are not repaired or replaced.)

bonus. Compensation over and above a party's base salary or wages. (Such payments are often based on performance, but are also sometimes used by small business owners as a method for reducing profits that will be realized by their companies.)

C

capital gain. Income that a taxpayer realizes when a capital asset is sold or exchanged for more than the taxpayer's basis in the asset.

capital loss. The difference between the value that a taxpayer receives in the sale or exchange of a capital asset and the taxpayer's basis in that asset when the sale or exchange occurs at a value that is less than the taxpayer's basis in the asset.

cash method of accounting. A system of income reporting that does not recognize income until receipts from a sale are actually received. Expenses incurred in connection with such sales are not recognized until they are actually paid.

commission. Compensation paid to a party for services rendered that is generally calculated on the basis of the party's performance. This commonly occurs in the form of a percentage of either the gross sale price or profit generated from the sale of a good or service.

cost of doing business. A term used to refer to the price incurred as a consequence of carrying on a given business enterprise. (Although it usually refers to the price in money, it may also include the sacrifice of alternative choices that must be made when one enterprise is chosen over others.)

D

deduction. A tax term used to refer to an amount of money that may be subtracted from a taxpayer's gross income in arriving at the party's taxable income.

deficit. A shortage in the amount of money that is required for some purpose.

dependency exemption. The right to take a prescribed amount of money as a tax deduction for purposes of arriving at taxable income due to having provided support for a party who is considered to be the taxpayer's dependent as provided by tax law.

dependent. A party for whom a taxpayer is entitled to take a dependency exemption, generally due to having provided more than half of the person's support for the tax year. The person may be deemed to be a taxpayer's dependent by agreement between divorced parents or among multiple parties who provide support for a person.

direct expense. Costs that are readily traceable to a particular activity or business venture.

direct tax. A levy specifically imposed on a given source of revenue or income.

dividends. Distributions of property or money made by corporations out of earnings and profits to their shareholders.

E

earned income. A taxpayer's total income from wages, salaries, and tips; net earnings from self-employment; or, gross income received as a statutory employee.

earned income credit. A type of welfare payment for those taxpayers whose earned incomes are beneath certain statutorily prescribed amounts. The purpose of the credit is to keep moderate income earners working, since they must have earned income in order to qualify for the credit.

employee. One who labors under the direction and control of another in exchange for wages, salary, or other compensation.

excise tax. A levy imposed by a governmental entity upon the sale or use of a good or service or upon the right to engage in certain occupations or activities.

exemptions. Allowances that entitle a taxpayer to exclude some statutorily prescribed amount of income from taxation. The allowances are generally based on the number of parties that the taxpayer provides support to including the taxpayer.

F

fair market value. The amount of money at which property or services would change hands in an arms-length transaction between unrelated parties.

federal income tax. A levy imposed by the federal government on earnings.

Federal Insurance Contributions Act (FICA) Tax. The combination of Old Age Security and Disability Income (OASDI) taxes and Medicare taxes that are assessed on the earnings of employees in the U.S. These must be withheld from workers' earnings by their employers and paid to the U.S. Treasury, along with a matching share paid by the employer.

filing status. One of five categories of individual taxpayers (single, married filing jointly, married filing separately, head of household, and qualifying widow or widower) that determine the level of income at which a taxpayer will be required and at what rate.

financial records. Written records that pertain to a party's money matters.

flat tax. A levy by a governmental entity on income or revenue whereby a single rate of taxation is applied on the entire amount that is subject to the levy.

form W-4 (Employee's Withholding Allowance Certificate). A federal tax form that employers must require their employees to complete indicating their number of dependents and basis for other withholding allowances thereby enabling the employer to determine how much income tax to withhold from each employee's earnings.

fringe benefits. Nonmonetary compensation provided to employees in addition to wages or salary. (Among the most common fringe benefits are health insurance, life insurance, and pension plans.)

G

gasoline excise tax. A levy by a governmental unit on gasoline used as fuel. The tax is usually imposed upon a party in the distribution chain and the tax is then added to the price of the gasoline as part of the sale price paid by the consumer, rather than as a direct tax paid by the consumer.

gross income. A party's total income from all sources before any allowances for exemptions or deductions from adjusted gross income.

H

head of household filing status. A taxpayer who is single and who provides a home and over half of the support for over half of the year to his or her child or to any relative (other than a cousin). Also, a taxpayer who is married, but has lived apart from his or her spouse for the last six months of the tax year and who has provided over half of the cost of maintaining a home for him- or herself and a dependent child for whom the party is entitled to claim a deduction as an exemption.

I

income taxes. A levy imposed by a governmental entity upon what it defines as the income. Generally, such entities define income to include wages, salaries, profits, gains from the sale of assets, and returns from investments.

independent contractor. One who performs work for others, but retains the right of control over how the work will be performed.

indirect expense. Costs that are not specifically related to a given transaction or venture, but which must be incurred to support the activity.

indirect tax. A levy by a governmental entity upon a good, service, or privilege that is imposed upon a party in the chain of distribution but which is then passed on to the consumer as a part of the price of what is sold.

inflation. A general increase in prices throughout a particular economy.

interest. A form of income that is payment by one party to another for the use of money.

interest income. Money received as compensation for the right to use one's money.

Internal Revenue Service (IRS). An agency within the U.S. Treasury Department that is charged with administration of the U.S. Internal Revenue Code.

investment income. Revenue generated as a result of ownership of assets that promise such payments as a reward for ownership. The most common types of investment income include interest and dividends.

K

keyman insurance. Life insurance and/or disability insurance taken out by an employer on employees who are of critical importance to the employer. The benefits of the policy accrue to the employer in order to provide the employer with funds to help offset the disruption caused by the death or disability of such an employee.

L

luxury tax. A levy imposed on the sale and/or purchase of goods or services that are considered frivolous. The tax may be imposed on the full sale price or merely on the part of the price that exceeds a certain exempt amount. The tax is often imposed to discourage consumption of a good or service.

M

married filing joint filing status. A category for filing a tax return that is available to married couples as long as they were married on the last day of the tax year and both elect such status. The filing status will determine whether or not the parties must file a return and their rates of taxation if they do file.

married filing separate filing status. A category for filing a tax return that is available to married couples. If either party of a married couple residing together chooses to file separately, both must. The status will determine if the parties must file a return and their rates of taxation if they do file.

Medicare tax. The portion of Federal Insurance Contributions Act (FICA) tax that is used to provide medical care primarily to the elderly. Unlike the Social Security part of FICA taxes, there is no limit to the amount of a party's income to which the Medicare part of FICA taxes applies.

modified adjusted gross income. A taxpayer's income remaining after certain additions are made to his or her adjusted gross income. Such adjustments will be prescribed for purposes of calculating a particular credit, deduction, or tax liability and they will be provided for in the instructions for making such calculations.

N

net operating loss (NOL). The degree to which a business operation's expenses exceed its business income for the tax year.

P

payroll taxes. Income taxes and Federal Insurance Contributions Act (FICA) tax withheld from the earnings of employees by their employers, as well as the matching share of FICA taxes that are paid by employers.

personal exemption. A statutorily provided allowance that a taxpayer is permitted to exclude from taxation. Personal exemptions are usually available to taxpayers for the parties for whom they provide support, including themselves.

personal identification number (PIN). A series of numbers, letters, or characters selected by a party that must be entered in able to access certain information or an account or in order to conduct certain business transactions.

phantom income. An amount of money that a party is deemed to have earned according to standard accounting practices, but which the party has not yet actually received.

progressive tax. A levy imposed upon income, revenue, or spending that is structured such that as the amount of money that is being taxed increases, the rate at which it is being taxed is increased at certain intervals.

property taxes. A levy imposed upon the realty or personal property that is owned, leased, or used by parties.

Q

qualifying child. A party who, by virtue of his or her age, relationship, income, and dependency, enables another party to qualify for certain tax advantages such as a dependency exemption, child credit, or earned income credit.

qualifying person. A party—other than a taxpayer's child—who, due to his or her relationship with or dependency upon a taxpayer, enables the taxpayer to be eligible for certain tax advantages.

qualifying widow(er) filing status. A category for filing a tax return available to a surviving spouse that permits him or her to use the married filing jointly rates for the year of the deceased spouse's death, and even the next two years if the surviving spouse has provided over half of the support for a qualifying child.

R

refund. Money paid to a taxpayer by a taxing authority due to overpayment of the party's tax obligation.

regressive tax. A levy imposed upon the income, revenue, or spending that is structured such that as the taxpayer's taxable base increases, the rate of tax levied on that base decreases.

rents. Payments made to the owner of rights in realty or personal property for the right to use that property.

resources. Assets of virtually any kind, including, but not limited to, money as well as the ability to meet future needs.

revenue. Income received.

S

salary. Payment to an employee as compensation for his or her employment that is often calculated without regard to hours spent on the job or actual work performed during the payment period but, rather, is calculated at a fixed rate.

sales tax. A levy imposed on the sale of goods and/or services. (Such taxes are usually calculated as a fixed percentage of the amount of the sale and are generally paid directly by the buyer.)

Section 1244 stock. Stock issued by a U.S. corporation whose capital and paid-in surplus at its inception did not exceed one million dollars; has not derived over 50% of its gross receipts of the past five years from passive income sources; and, whose stock is owned by either an individual or partnership to whom it was issued at its inception.

self-employment tax. A levy imposed upon those who earn income through self-employment as a replacement for the Federal Insurance Contributions Act (FICA) tax that is paid by employees and their employers.

single filing status. A category for filing a tax return available to those who are unmarried on the last day of the tax year.

Social Security tax. The portion of Federal Insurance Contributions Act (FICA) tax that is used to finance retirement benefits for the aged, disability benefits for the disabled, and survivors benefits for dependent children of deceased taxpayers. It is also referred to as Old Age Security and Disability Income (OASDI) tax.

standard deduction. An amount set by Congress that taxpayers may exclude from taxation without having to offer any proof as to the amount of expenditures to support the deduction. (The standard deduction is a simplified alternative to itemizing deductions.)

T

tax code. A compilation of laws by a governmental entity that mandate the payment of levies to that entity by those over whom it has jurisdiction.

tax credit. An allowance that can be used to offset tax liability on a dollar-for-dollar basis.

tax credits. The sum total of each tax credit that a taxpayer is allowed to take. Some tax credits are permitted to generate tax refunds (refundable credits), whereas others can be used only to the extent that they offset tax liability (nonrefundable credits). Some can be carried to other years and some cannot.

tax liability. The amount of money that a party owes as the result of the levy of some tax upon him or her.

tax shelters. Activities that are designed to produce tax deductions and credits that may be used to offset regular taxable income.

taxable interest income. The portion of money received for allowing another party to use one's money that is subject to taxation.

taxes. Mandatory levies imposed by a governmental entity upon those over which it has jurisdiction.

tax-exempt interest income. That portion of funds received for allowing another party to use one's money that is not subject to taxation.

telefile. A paperless method of filing a tax return by telephone.

tentative minimum tax. An intermediate figure arrived at in the process of calculating a taxpayer's alternative minimum tax. It consists of the taxpayer's alternative minimum tax before deducting the party's federal tax liability, less foreign tax credits and taxes paid on lump sum distributions from qualified plans.

tip income. Payment given to a party for personal services that were rendered. Typical of such payments are those made to waiters and waitresses.

W

wages. Payments made to an employee as compensation for his or her employment. (Such payments are generally made on the basis of the number of hours that the employee has spent on the job during the pay period.)

withholding. Money held out of an employee's compensation by his or her employer that are to be paid to the U.S. Treasury by the employer in order to enable the employee to meet his or her obligation to pay income taxes and the Federal Insurance Contributions Act (FICA) tax.

Appendix A

IRS Form 656, Offer in Compromise

This Appendix contains parts of IRS Form 656, Offer in Compromise. This is provided so you may refer to it as you are reading the text. For the full form, go to the IRS website at **www.irs.gov**, or call 800-829-1040.

NOTE: *New legislation, the Tax Increase Prevention and Reconciliation Act of 2005 (TIPRA), has created significant changes to the Offer in Compromise Program. Particularly, TIPRA made major changes to the requirements for submitting lump-sum and periodic-payment offers. In addition to the $150 application fee, you must also include 20% of your offer amount if you propose a cash or lump-sum offer (a cash or lump-sum offer is an offer you propose to pay in five (5) or less payments); or, you must also include a payment equal to your first proposed offer amount and you must pay the remaining proposed payments when they are due. Failure to meet these new requirements will result in the return of your offer as not processable.*

Department of the Treasury
Internal Revenue Service

www.irs.gov

Form 656 (Rev. 7-2004)
Catalog Number 16728N

Form 656

Offer in Compromise

IMPORTANT! THIS BOOKLET CONTAINS INFORMATION THAT YOU NEED IN ORDER TO PREPARE A COMPLETE AND ACCURATE OFFER IN COMPROMISE. *PLEASE READ THESE INSTRUCTIONS CAREFULLY BEFORE ATTEMPTING TO COMPLETE THE ENCLOSED FORMS.*

CONTENTS

Note: If you have any questions, please call our toll-free number at 1–800–829–1040. You can get forms and publications by calling toll free at 1–800–829–3676 (1–800–TAX–FORM), or by visiting your local Internal Revenue Service (IRS) office or our website at *www.irs.gov*.

What is an Offer in Compromise?

An Offer in Compromise *(OIC)* is an agreement between the taxpayer and the government that settles a tax liability for payment of less than the full amount owed.

The Service will generally accept an OIC when it is unlikely that the tax liability can be collected in full and the amount offered reasonably reflects collection potential. An OIC is a legitimate alternative to declaring a case currently not collectible or to a "protracted installment agreement." The goal is to achieve collection of what is potentially collectible at the earliest possible time and at the least cost to the government.

Note: A "protracted installment agreement" is defined as being one that extends beyond the period allowed under IRS issued guidelines.

The success of the Offer in Compromise program will be assured only if taxpayers make adequate compromise proposals consistent with their ability to pay and the Service makes prompt and reasonable decisions. Taxpayers are expected to provide reasonable documentation to verify their ability to pay. The ultimate goal is a compromise which is in the best interest of *both* the taxpayer and the Service. Acceptance of an adequate offer will also result in creating for the taxpayer an expectation of, and a fresh start toward, compliance with all future filing and payment requirements.

■ *Doubt as to Collectibility*. Doubt exists that you could **ever** pay the full amount of tax owed. Before the IRS can consider a **doubt as to collectibility** offer *(absent special circumstances)*, the taxpayer *must not* be able to pay the taxes in full either by liquidating assets or through current installment agreement guidelines. You *must* submit the appropriate collection information statement along with all required supporting documents.

■ *Doubt as to Liability*. This means that doubt exists that the assessed tax is correct. **Do not use this reason if the sole basis for filing an offer is because you are unable to pay the tax liability.** If you do not think that you owe the tax liability, then you may submit an OIC for **"Doubt as to Liability"** *(see Item 6 on Form 656)*. You *must* submit a detailed written statement explaining why you believe you do not owe the tax that you want to compromise. You are not required to submit a collection information statement if you are submitting an offer on this basis alone.

■ *Effective Tax Administration (ETA).* This means that the taxpayer **does not have any doubt** that the tax is correct and there is **no doubt** that the full amount of tax owed could be collected, but an exceptional circumstance exists that would allow us to consider your offer. To be eligible for compromise on this basis, you must demonstrate that the collection of the tax would create an economic hardship or would be unfair and inequitable. If you are requesting an ETA offer, you *must* submit:

1. A collection information statement with all appropriate attachments, and

2. A written narrative explaining your special circumstances and why paying the tax liability in full would create an economic hardship or would be unfair and inequitable.

You *must* also attach appropriate documentation that will support your request for an ETA offer such as proof of unusual expenses that would cause you economic hardship if the taxes were collected in full.

The information in this package is designed to assist you in determining if an offer in compromise is the right payment option for you, as well as guide you through the process of completing a complete offer in compromise application package. *Please read and follow the directions carefully!*

1

Step One: Is Your Offer in Compromise (OIC) "Processable?"

(Note: The three questions below do not apply if your offer is based only on doubt as to liability.)

PLEASE DO NOT GO ANY FURTHER WITHOUT FIRST DETERMINING WHETHER OR NOT YOU ARE ELIGIBLE TO HAVE YOUR OFFER IN COMPROMISE PROCESSED AT THIS TIME.

In order to determine whether or not you are eligible to have your offer in compromise processed, please answer the 3 questions below:

	YES	NO
1. Do you currently have an open bankruptcy proceeding? You should contact your Bankruptcy Attorney if you are not certain. If you are involved in an open bankruptcy proceeding, contact your local IRS insolvency office. Any resolution of your outstanding tax liabilities generally must take place within the context of your bankruptcy proceeding.	☐	☐
2. Do you have any unfiled federal tax returns that you are **required** to file? You **must** file all tax returns that you were legally required to file prior to submitting an offer in compromise. This includes but is not limited to:	☐	☐

- All Income Tax, Employment Tax, and Excise Tax returns, along with all required Partnership, Limited Liability Corporations, or closely held Sub-Chapter S Corporation returns.

If you did not file a return for a specific year prior to submitting your OIC because you were not legally required to file the return, then you **must** include a detailed explanation of your circumstances with your OIC.

| 3. If you are a business with employees, have you failed to *timely* make any required federal tax deposits for the current quarter and the two immediate preceding quarters? *(If you have any untimely federal tax deposits for the above quarters or late filing of returns, then you must answer yes to this question.)* | ☐ | ☐ |

If you answered YES to any of the questions above, STOP HERE. You are *not eligible* to have your offer considered or processed at this time. If you answered NO to all of the questions above, then you *may be eligible* to have your offer considered and processed.

Additional Requirements

1. ***Offer in Compromise Application Fee*** — Your offer must include the $150 application fee or a completed Form 656-A, *Income Certification of Offer in Compromise Application Fee*, if you are requesting an exception of the fee because of your income. Offers received without the $150 fee or a completed Form 656-A will not be accepted for processing. Please see Step 5 on Page 13 of this package for more information on the application fee and to determine if you qualify for the exception.

2. You **must** use the current versions of Form 656, *Offer in Compromise*, and Form 433-A and Form 433-B, Collection Information Statements, which are contained in this package.

- Individual or Self-Employed taxpayers must use Form 433-A, *Collection Information Statement for Wage Earners and Self-Employed Individuals*.

- Corporations and other business taxpayers must use Form 433-B, *Collection Information Statement for Businesses*. We may also require Form 433-A from corporate officers or individual partners.

- **Offers received on outdated forms or without the required information statements will not be considered**.

2

Step Two: What We Need to Fully Evaluate Your Offer

1. COMPLETE AN ACCURATE FORM 656 — Complete all applicable items on Form 656, **which is the official compromise agreement**. You **must** sign Form 656. If someone other than yourself prepared the offer package, then please see the instructions in Step Four, Items 12 and 13, found on Page 11 of this package. If your Form 656 was prepared by an authorized Representative, you **must** include a completed Form 2848, *Power of Attorney and Declaration of Representative*, with your offer. Detailed instructions for the completion of Form 656 are found on Pages 10 and 11 of this package.

Common errors to avoid in completing Form 656:

- The taxpayer's name is missing.

- The street address is missing or incomplete.

- The social security number *(SSN)* or employer identification number *(EIN)* is missing, incomplete, or incorrect.

- The preprinted terms and conditions listed on the Form 656 have been altered or deleted.

- An offer amount or payment term is missing.

- A required signature is missing.

2. COMPLETE AN ACCURATE COLLECTION INFORMATION STATEMENT (Form 433-A and/or Form 433-B) — You **must** provide financial information when you submit offers based on doubt as to collectibility and effective tax administration. **We do not require this information if your offer is based solely on doubt as to liability.** You **must** send us current information that reflects your financial situation for the **three months** immediately prior to the date you submitted your offer in compromise. Collection information statements **must** show all of your assets and income, even those unavailable to us through direct collection action, because you can possibly use them to fund your offer. The offer examiner needs this information to evaluate your offer and may ask you to update it or verify certain financial information. These forms **must** be filled in completely. We may return offer packages that are incomplete. Annotate items that do not apply to you with "N/A." **Provide all the information required to support your financial condition.** Required items of documentation are clearly indicated on the collection information statements with icons.

When only one spouse has a tax liability but both have incomes, only the spouse responsible for the tax debt is required to prepare the necessary collection information statements. The responsible spouse should include **only** his/her assets and liabilities on his/her collection information statements. However, the income and expenses of the entire household is required on their collection information statements. The entire household includes spouse, domestic partner, significant other, children, and others that contribute to the household. This is necessary for the IRS to evaluate the income and expenses allocable to the liable taxpayer.

In States with community property laws, we require collection information statements from both spouses. We may also require financial information on the non-liable spouse, or cohabitant(s), for offer verification purposes, even when community property laws do not apply.

3

3. RESPOND PROMPTLY TO REQUESTS FOR ADDITIONAL INFORMATION — While we are evaluating your offer, we may contact you for any information that is missing, or requires clarification. Respond promptly to any requests for additional information. **If we do not receive this information from you in a timely manner, we will not give your offer any further consideration. It will be returned to you, and** *you will forfeit the $150 application fee.*

4. ESTIMATED TAX PAYMENTS MUST BE UP TO DATE FOR THE CURRENT YEAR — We will not process your offer to completion if we determine that your estimated tax payments for the current year's income tax liability are not paid up to date. If we determine this to be the case, you will have one opportunity to make the required payments before we return your offer. If we return your offer because you did not make the estimated tax payments, then your $150 application fee will be forfeited.

Step Three: Determining the Amount of Your Offer

Doubt as to Collectibility

Your offer amount must equal or exceed your reasonable collection potential amount. The information provided on the collection information statements *(Form 433-A and Form 433-B)* assists us in determining the reasonable collection potential *(RCP)* of your tax liability. The RCP equals the net equity of your assets plus the amount we could collect from your future income. **If our financial analysis indicates that you have the ability to fully pay the tax liability, either immediately or through an installment agreement, unless special circumstances are involved, your offer will not be accepted. You must offer an amount greater than or equal to the RCP amount. All offer amounts must exceed zero, including doubt as to liability offers.**

If special circumstances cause you to offer an amount less than the RCP, you *must* complete Item 9, "Explanation of Circumstances," on Form 656, explaining your situation. You *must* also attach to Form 656 any supporting documents to help support your special circumstances. Special circumstances may include factors such as advanced age, serious illness from which recovery is unlikely, or any other factors that impact upon

your ability to pay the total RCP and continue to provide for the necessary living expenses for you and your family.

If you are a wage earner or self-employed individual, completion of the worksheet on Pages 8 and 9 will give you a good estimate of what an acceptable offer amount may be. You will use the information on your Form 433-A to complete the worksheet.

Doubt as to Liability

Complete Item 9, "Explanation of Circumstances," on Form 656, explaining why, in your judgment, you do not owe the tax liability you want to compromise. Offer the correct tax, penalty, and interest owed based on your judgment in Item 7 on Form 656.

Effective Tax Administration (ETA)

Complete Form 433-A or Form 433-B, as appropriate, and attach to Form 656. You *must* complete Item 9, "Explanation of Circumstances," on Form 656, explaining your exceptional circumstances and why requiring payment of the tax liability in full would either create an economic hardship or would be unfair and inequitable. You *must* also attach to Form 656 any documents to help support your exceptional circumstances.

Determine Your Payment Terms

There are three payment plans you and the IRS may agree to:

- **Cash** *(paid in 90 days or less)*;

- **Short-Term Deferred Payment** *(more than 90 days, up to 24 months)*;

- **Deferred Payment** *(offers with payment terms over the remaining statutory period for collecting the tax).*

Cash Offer

You must pay cash offers within 90 days of a written notice of acceptance.

You should offer the realizable value of your assets plus the total amount we could collect over 48 months of payments *(or the remainder of the ten-year statutory period for collection, whichever is less).*

Note: We require full payment of accepted doubt as to liability offers at the time of mutual agreement of the corrected liability. If you're unable to pay the corrected amount, you must also request compromise on the basis of doubt as to collectibility.

Short-Term Deferred Payment Offer

This payment plan requires you to pay the offer within two years of acceptance.

The offer must include the realizable value of your assets plus the amount we could collect over 60 months of payments *(or the remainder of the ten-year statutory period for collection, whichever is less).*

You can pay the short-term deferred payment plan in three ways:

Plan One

- Full payment of the realizable value of your assets within 90 days from the date we accept your offer, and

- Payment within two years of acceptance of the amount we could collect over 60 months *(future income)* or the remaining life of the collection statute, whichever is less.

Plan Two

- Cash payment for a portion of the realizable value of your assets within 90 days from the date we accept your offer, and

- The balance of the realizable value plus the amount we could collect over 60 months *(future income)* or the remaining life of the collection statute, whichever is less, within two years of acceptance.

Plan Three

- The entire offer amount in monthly payments extending over a period not to exceed two years from date of acceptance *(e.g., four payments within 120 days of acceptance).*

For example, on a short-term deferred payment total offer of $16,000, you might propose to pay your realizable value of assets *(e.g., $13,000)* within 90 days of acceptance and the amount of your future income *(e.g., $50 per month for 60 months, or $3,000)* over 6 monthly payments of $500 each, beginning the first month after acceptance.

We may file a Notice of Federal Tax Lien on tax liabilities compromised under short-term payment offers.

6

Deferred Payment Offer

This payment plan requires you to pay the offer amount over the remaining statutory period for collecting the tax.

The offer must include the realizable value of your assets plus the amount we could collect through monthly payments during the remaining life of the collection statute.

■ Using the worksheet on Pages 8 and 9, multiply the amount from Item 12, Box O, by the number of months remaining on the collection statute. Add that amount to Item 11, Box N, and use the total as the basis for your offer amount in Item 7 of Form 656.

You can pay the deferred payment plan in three ways:

Plan One

■ Full payment of the realizable value of your assets within 90 days from the date we accept your offer, and

■ Your "future income" in monthly payments during the remaining life of the collection statute

Plan Two

■ Cash payment for a portion of the realizable value of your assets within 90 days from the date we accept your offer, and

■ Monthly payments during the remaining life of the collection statute for both the balance of the realizable value and your future income

Plan Three

■ The entire offer amount in monthly payments over the life of the collection statute

For example, on a deferred payment offer with 7 years *(84 months)* remaining on the statutory period for collection and a total offer of $25,000, you might propose to pay your realizable value of assets *(e.g., $10,000)* within 90 days and your future income *(e.g., $179 per month for 7 years, or $15,000)* in 84 monthly installments of $179. Alternately, you could also pay the same total $25,000 offer in 84 monthly installments of $298.

Just as with short-term deferred payment offers, we may file a Notice of Federal Tax Lien on tax liabilities compromised under Deferred Payment Offers.

Note: The worksheet on Pages 8 and 9 instructs wage earners and self-employed individuals how to figure the appropriate amount for a Cash, Short-Term Deferred Payment, or Deferred Payment Offer.

Offer in Compromise Worksheet

Please see Pages 8 and 9.

Funding Your Offer

If you do not have the cash to pay your offer amount immediately, you should begin the process of exploring options to finance your offer amount. Options you may want to consider include liquidating assets, obtaining a loan from a lending institution, borrowing on your home equity through a second mortgage or reverse mortgage, or borrowing funds from family members or friends.

Worksheet to Calculate an Offer Amount
For use by Wage Earners and Self-Employed Individuals.

Keep this worksheet for your records.
Do not send to IRS.

Use this Worksheet to calculate an offer amount using information from Form 433-A.

1. Enter total checking accounts from Item 11c

   A

2. Enter total other accounts from Item 12c

   B

   If less than 0 , enter 0

3. Enter total investments from Item 13d

   C

4. Enter total cash on hand from Item 14a

   D

5. Enter life insurance cash value from Item 16f

   E

6. Enter total accounts/notes receivable from Item 23m

   F

   Subtotal: Add boxes A through F = | G

---

7. Purchased Automobiles, Trucks, and Other Licensed Assets

	Enter current value for each asset		Enter loan balance for each asset	Individual asset value (if less than 0 , enter 0)
From line 18a	$	x .8 = $	—$	=
From line 18b	$	x .8 = $	—$	=
From line 18c	$	x .8 = $	—$	=

Subtotal = | H

---

8. Real Estate

	Enter current value for each asset		Enter loan balance for each asset	Individual asset value (if less than 0 , enter 0)
From line 20a	$	x .8 = $	—$	=
From line 20b	$	x .8 = $	—$	=

Subtotal = | I

---

9. Personal Assets

	Enter current value for each asset		Enter loan balance for each asset	Individual asset value (if less than 0 , enter 0)
From line 21b	$	x .8 = $	—$	=
From line 21c	$	x .8 = $	—$	=
From line 21d	$	x .8 = $	—$	=
From line 21e	$	x .8 = $	—$	=

Subtotal = | J

| From line 21a | $ | x .8 = $ | —$ | = |

Subtract —$ 7040.00

Subtotal = | K

---

10. Business Assets

	Enter current value for each asset		Enter loan balance for each asset	Individual asset value (if less than 0 , enter 0)
From line 22b	$	x .8 = $	—$	=
From line 22c	$	x .8 = $	—$	=
From line 22d	$	x .8 = $	—$	=
From line 22e	$	x .8 = $	—$	=

Subtotal = | L

| From line 22a | $ | x .8 = $ | —$ | = |

Subtract —$ 3520.00

Subtotal = | M

8

11. Add amounts in Boxes G through M to obtain your total equity and assets   =   [N]

12. Enter amount from Item 34 $_____

Enter amount from Item 45 and subtract   — $_____

      Net Difference   =   [O]

This amount would be available
to pay monthly on your tax liability.

If Box O is 0 or less, STOP. Use
the amount from Box N and to base
your offer amount in Item 7 of Form
656. **Your offer amount must equal
or exceed (*) the amount shown in
Box N.**

13a.

If you will pay the offer amount
in 90 days or less (i.e., cash offer):

Enter amount
from Box O $ _____

Multiply by   **x 48**
(or the number of months
remaining on the ten-year
statutory period for collection,
whichever is less)

  =   [P]

Enter amount
from Box N   +   [Q]

Add amounts
in Box P and   =   [R]
Box Q

**Use the amount
from Box R to base
your offer amount
in Item 7 of Form
656.
Note: Your offer
amount must equal
or exceed (*) the
amount shown in
Box R.**

13b.

If you will pay the offer amount in more
than 90 days but less than 2 years
(i.e., short-term deferred payment offer):

Enter amount
from Box O $ _____

Multiply by   **x 60**
(or the number of months
remaining on the ten-year
statutory period for collection,
whichever is less)

  =   [S]

Enter amount
from Box N   +   [T]

Add amounts
in Box S and   =   [U]
Box T

**Use the amount
from Box U to base
your offer amount
in Item 7 of Form
656.
Note: Your offer
amount must equal
or exceed (*) the
amount shown in
Box U.**

Note: Do not compute your offer amount using 13a or 13b if your
statute expiration date(s) is less than 5 years from the date of your
offer. Instead, refer to page 5 under Deferred Payment Offer options
1 through 3.

* Unless you are submitting an offer under effective tax administration or doubt as to collectibility
with special circumstances considerations, as described on page 4.

9

Step Four: Completing Form 656, Offer in Compromise

We have included two *Offer in Compromise* forms. Use one form to submit your *Offer in Compromise*. You may use the other form as a worksheet and retain it for your personal records.

Note: If you have any questions about completing this form, you may call toll free at 1–800–829–1040 or visit your local IRS office or our website at www.irs.gov. We may return your offer if you don't follow these instructions.

Item 1: Enter your name and home or business street address. Show **both names** on a joint offer for joint liabilities. You also should include a mailing address if it is different from your street address.

If you owe a liability —

Jointly with another person and **both of you agree** to submit an offer, send only **one** Form 656, *Offer in Compromise, and* **one** $150 application fee *(or Form 656-A, if applicable).*

By yourself *(such as employment taxes),* and other liabilities with another person *(such as income taxes),* but **only you** are submitting an offer, then list **all** tax liabilities on **one** Form 656 and submit **one** $150 application fee *(or Form 656-A, if applicable).*

By yourself and another one jointly, and **both of you** submit an offer, then you must show **all** tax liabilities on your Form 656 and submit **one** $150 application fee *(or Form 656-A, if applicable).* **The other person** should show *only* the joint tax liability on their Form 656 and submit **one** $150 application fee *(of Form 656-A, if applicable).*

Item 2: Enter the social security number(s) for the person(s) submitting the offer. For example, enter the social security number of both spouses when submitting a joint offer for a joint tax liability. However, when only one spouse submits an offer, enter only that spouse's social security number.

Item 3: Enter the employer identification number for offers from businesses.

Item 4: Show the employer identification numbers for all other businesses *(excluding corporate entities)* that you own or in which you have an ownership interest.

Item 5: Identify your tax liability and enter the tax year or period. Letters and notices from us and Notices of Federal Tax Lien show the tax periods for trust fund recovery penalties.

Item 6: Check the appropriate box(es) describing the basis for your offer.

Doubt as to Liability offers require a statement describing in detail why you think you do not owe the liability. Complete Item 9, "Explanation of Circumstances," explaining your situation.

Doubt as to Collectibility offers require you to complete a Form 433-A, *Collection Information Statement for Wage Earners and Self-Employed Individuals*, if you are an individual taxpayer, or a Form 433-B, *Collection Information Statement for Businesses*, if you are a corporation or other business taxpayer.

Note: Attach to the upper left corner of Form 656 the six (6) pages of the collection information statement(s) and all related documents before you send it to us.

10

Item 6 *(cont'd)*:	**Effective Tax Administration** offers require you to complete a Form 433-A, *Collection Information Statement for Wage Earners and Self-Employed Individuals,* if you are an individual	taxpayer, or a Form 433-B, *Collection Information Statement for Businesses,* if you are a corporation or other business taxpayer. Complete Item 9, "Explanation of Circumstances."
Item 7:	Enter the total amount of your offer *(see Page 5, "Determining the Amount of Your Offer").* Your offer amount cannot include a refund we owe you or amounts you have already paid.	Check the appropriate payment box *(cash, short-term deferred payment or deferred payment — see Page 6, "Determine Your Payment Terms")* and describe your payment plan in the spaces provided.
Item 8:	It is important that you understand the requirements listed in this section. Pay particular attention to Items 8(d)	and 8(g), as they address the future compliance provision and refunds.
Item 9:	Explain your reason*(s)* for submitting your offer in the "Explanation of Circumstances." You may attach	additional sheets if necessary. Include your name and SSN or EIN on all attachments.
Item 10:	Explain where you will get the funds to pay the amount you are offering.	
Item 11:	11(a) and 11(b) **Signature of Taxpayer.** All persons submitting the offer must sign and date Form 656. Include titles of	authorized corporate officers, executors, trustees, Powers of Attorney, etc., where applicable.
Item 12:	If someone other than the taxpayer prepared this Offer in Compromise, the	taxpayer should insert their name and address *(if known)* in Item 12.
Item 13:	Paid Preparer's Use Only. Self explanatory.	Please see the "Privacy Act Notice" on Page 13.
Item 14:	If you want to allow the IRS to discuss your Offer in Compromise with a friend, family member, or any other person, including an individual you paid to prepare this form, check the "Yes" box in Item 14, "Third Party Designee," on your Form 656. Also enter the designee's name and phone number. Checking the "Yes" box allows the IRS to contact another person and discuss with that person any additional information	the IRS needs to process your offer. This additional information may include information about tax liabilities you failed to list in Item 5 on your Form 656 or returns you have failed to file. If your contact person is an attorney, CPA, or enrolled agent and you wish to have them represent you regarding this offer, a Form 2848, *Power of Attorney and Declaration of Representative,* should be completed and submitted with your offer.

Note: *Staple in the upper left corner the four (4) pages of Form 656 before you send it to us.*

Privacy Act Notice

We ask for the information on this form to carry out the internal revenue laws of the United States. Our authority to request this information is section 7801. Our purpose for requesting the information is to determine if it is in the best interests of the IRS to accept an offer in compromise. You are not required to make an offer in compromise; however, if you choose to do so, you must provide all of the taxpayer information requested. Failure to provide all of the information may prevent us from processing your request. If you are a paid preparer and you prepared the Form 656 for the taxpayer submitting an offer, we request that you complete and sign Item 13 on Form 656, and provide identifying information. Providing this information is voluntary. This information will be used to administer and enforce the internal revenue laws of the United States and may be used to regulate practice before the Internal Revenue Service for those persons subject to Treasury Department Circular No. 230, *Regulations Governing the Practice of Attorneys, Certified Public Accountants, Enrolled Agents, Enrolled Actuaries, and Appraisers before the Internal Revenue Service.* Information on this form may be disclosed to the Department of Justice for civil and criminal litigation. We may also disclose this information to cities, states, and the District of Columbia for use in administering their tax laws, and to Federal and state agencies to enforce nontax criminal laws and to combat terrorism. The authority to disclose information to combat terrorism expired on December 31, 2003. However, legislation is pending that would reinstate this authority. Providing false or fraudulent information on this form may subject you to criminal prosecution and penalties.

Step Five: Offer in Compromise *(OIC)* Application Fee

What is an Offer in Compromise Application Fee?	When you submit an offer in compromise *(OIC)*, the Internal Revenue Service expends resources evaluating your individual financial condition. The OIC	application fee allows the Internal Revenue Service to recover a portion of the cost of processing your OIC.
How much is the fee?	The application fee is $150 for each Form 656 submitted. **Do not send cash.** Please pay either by check or money order and make payable to the	"**United States Treasury.**" *(See Offer in Compromise (OIC) Application Fee Worksheet.)*
When is the fee due?	The application fee of $150 is due at the time you submit your OIC for consideration.	
Do all OICs require this fee?	You must remit the application fee along with your Form 656, *Offer in Compromise*, **unless**: (1) Your OIC is based solely on **doubt as to liability** *(see Page 1 of this Offer in Compromise package)*, **or** (2) You certify that your total monthly income is at or below levels based on the poverty guidelines established by the	U.S. Department of Health and Human Services. *(See Offer in Compromise (OIC) Application Fee Worksheet.)* The exception for taxpayers with incomes below these levels only applies to individuals; it does not apply to other entities such as corporations or partnerships.
How do I determine if I qualify for the exception?	To determine if you qualify for the exception, please complete the attached Offer in Compromise *(OIC)* Application Fee Worksheet.	
Is the application fee ever refunded?	If the Internal Revenue Service accepts your OIC based on effective tax administration or special circumstances *(see Pages 1 and 5, respectively, in this Offer in Compromise package)*, the fee will be applied against the amount of the offer, or refunded to you if you	request. In addition, if your offer is determined to be **not** processable as described on Page 2 of this Offer in Compromise package, then your $150 application fee will be returned to you along with your offer.
What happens if I do not submit the application fee with my OIC Form 656?	Except for the two situations described above under "Do all OICs require this fee?" any OIC submitted without the	fee will be returned to you without further consideration.
Where do I call if I have additional questions about OICs and the application fee?	If you have additional questions about an OIC or about the application fee, please call toll free at 1–800–829–1040 or visit our website at *www.irs.gov*.	

Step Six: Where You Need to Send Your Offer

Where to File IF YOU RESIDE IN

The states of Alaska, Alabama, Arizona, California, Colorado, Hawaii, Idaho, Kentucky, Louisiana, Mississippi, Montana, Nevada, New Mexico, Oregon, Tennessee, Texas, Utah, Washington, Wisconsin or Wyoming,

AND	AND
You are a wage earner, retiree, or a self-employed individual without employees,	You are **OTHER** than a wage earner, retiree, or a self-employed individual without employees,
THEN MAIL	THEN MAIL
Form 656 and attachments to:	Form 656 and attachments to:
Memphis Internal Revenue Service Center COIC Unit **PO Box 30803, AMC** Memphis, TN 38130-0803	Memphis Internal Revenue Service Center COIC Unit **PO Box 30804, AMC** Memphis, TN 38130-0804

IF YOU RESIDE IN

Arkansas, Connecticut, Delaware, District of Columbia, Florida, Georgia, Illinois, Indiana, Iowa, Kansas, Maine, Maryland, Massachusetts, Michigan, Minnesota, Missouri, Nebraska, New Hampshire, New Jersey, New York, North Carolina, North Dakota, Ohio, Oklahoma, Pennsylvania, Puerto Rico, Rhode Island, South Carolina, South Dakota, Vermont, Virginia, West Virginia or have a foreign address,

AND	AND
You are a wage earner, retiree, or a self-employed individual without employees,	You are **OTHER** than a wage earner, retiree, or a self-employed individual without employees,
THEN MAIL	THEN MAIL
Form 656 and attachments to:	Form 656 and attachments to:
Brookhaven Internal Revenue Service Center COIC Unit **PO Box 9007** Holtsville, NY 11742-9007	Brookhaven Internal Revenue Service Center COIC Unit **PO Box 9008** Holtsville, NY 11742-9008

14

Step Seven: What to Expect after the IRS Receives Your Offer

How We Consider Your Offer

An offer examiner will evaluate your offer and may request additional documentation from you to verify financial or other information you provide. The examiner will then make a recommendation to accept or reject the offer. The examiner may also return your offer if you don't provide the requested information.

The examiner may decide that a larger offer amount is necessary to justify acceptance. You will have the opportunity to amend your offer.

Additional Agreements

When you submit certain offers, we may also request that you sign an additional agreement requiring you to:

- Pay a percentage of your future earnings.
- Waive certain present or future tax benefits.

Withholding Collection Activities

There are certain circumstances where we will withhold collection activities while we consider your offer. We will not act to collect the tax liability:

- While we investigate and evaluate your offer.

- For 30 days after we reject an offer.

- While you appeal an offer rejection.

- **However, a Notice of Federal Tax Lien may be filed at any time while your offer is being considered.**

The above do not apply if we find any indication that you submitted your offer to delay collection or cause a delay which will jeopardize our ability to collect the tax.

If you currently have an installment agreement when you submit an offer, you must continue making the agreed upon monthly payments while we consider your offer.

If We Accept Your Offer

If we accept your offer, we will notify you by mail. When you receive your acceptance letter, you must:

- Promptly pay any unpaid amounts that become due under the terms of the offer agreement. You must comply with the payment terms specified in the agreement in a timely manner or your offer and agreement will be in default.

- Comply with all the terms and conditions of the offer, along with those of any additional agreement.

- Promptly notify us of any change of address until you meet the conditions of your offer. Your acceptance letter will indicate the IRS office to contact if your address changes. Your notification allows us to contact you immediately regarding the status of your offer.

We will release all Notices of Federal Tax Lien when you satisfy the payment terms of the offered amount. For an immediate release of a lien, you can submit certified funds with a request letter to the address on the acceptance letter.

Once your offer is accepted, not filing returns or paying taxes when due could result in the default of an accepted offer *(see Item 8(d) of Form 656 for the future compliance provision).* If you default your agreement, we will reinstate the unpaid amount of the original tax liability, file a Notice of Federal Tax Lien on any tax liability without a filed notice, and resume collection activities. The future compliance provision applies to offers based on **doubt as to collectibility**. In certain cases, the future compliance provision may apply to offers based on **effective tax administration**.

We will not default your offer agreement when you have filed a joint offer with your spouse or ex-spouse as long as you have kept or are keeping all the terms of the agreement, even if your spouse or ex-spouse violates the future compliance provision.

Except for offers based on **doubt as to liability**, the offer agreement requires you to forego certain refunds, and to return those refunds to us if they are issued to you by mistake. These conditions are also listed on Form 656, Items 8(g) and 8(h). For example, if your offer was accepted by the IRS in the tax year 2004, the IRS would keep the refund due to you with respect to the tax year 2004, which you would normally receive in calendar year 2005 *(because the due date for filing the tax year 2004 is April 15, 2005).*

If We Reject Your Offer

We'll notify you by mail if we reject your offer. In our letter, we will explain our reason for the rejection. We will also keep your $150 application fee. If your offer is rejected, you have the right to:

■ Appeal our decision to the Office of Appeals within thirty days from the date of our letter. The letter will include detailed instructions on how to appeal the rejection.

■ Submit another offer with another application fee. You must increase an offer we've rejected as being too low when your financial situation remains unchanged. However, you must provide updated financial information when your financial situation has changed or when the original offer is more than six months old.

Step Eight: Offer in Compromise *(OIC)* Summary Checklist

Below is a checklist of items that you should review and complete prior to submitting your Form 656, *Offer in Compromise.* This checklist is solely for your benefit, so do not submit with your offer.

❏ Did you answer YES to any of the three questions on Page 2? If you did, then please do not submit Form 656 because you are not eligible to have your offer considered at this time.

❏ Have you properly completed Form 656, *Offer in Compromise,* by following the instructions on Pages 10 and 11?

❏ The preprinted terms and conditions listed on Form 656 have not changed.

❏ Are you using the most current versions of Form 656, Form 433-A, and Form 433-B as instructed on Page 2.

❏ You included your name *(or names, if joint).*

❏ You included your social security number *(SSN)* or employer identification number *(EIN)* and it is accurate.

❏ You included an offer amount *(the amount must be greater than zero)* or payment term.

❏ You signed the Form 656. If this is a joint Form 656, both spouses must sign Form 656.

❏ **You either attached the application fee in the designated area on the Form 656 or attached the Form 656-A certification, whichever is applicable.** If you attached Form 656-A, then you *must* complete the Offer in Compromise *(OIC)* Application Fee Worksheet.

❏ If your offer is based on **doubt as to collectibility,** you included complete financial information *(Form 433-A or Form 433-B, or both)* and all attachments.

❏ You signed or initialed in all required places on Form 433-A and/or Form 433-B.

❏ Your offer amount is greater than or equal to the reasonable collection potential *(RCP)* as described on Page 5 and calculated on Page 9.

❏ If applicable, are Items 12 and 14, on Form 656 completed?

❏ If applicable, is Item 13 on Form 656 completed and **signed?**

❏ Have you properly identified where to file your Form 656 from the instructions on Page 14?

If you have any questions, please call our toll-free number at 1–800–829–1040. You can get forms and publications by calling toll free at 1–800–829–3676 (1–800–TAX–FORM), or by visiting your local Internal Revenue Service (IRS) office or our website at *www.irs.gov.*

Important Information Regarding the Offer in Compromise *(OIC)*

Statute of Limitations for Collection is Suspended — The statute of limitations for collection of a tax debt is suspended while an OIC is "pending," or being reviewed. The Offer in Compromise is pending starting with the date an authorized IRS employee determines the Form 656, *Offer in Compromise*, can be processed and signs the Form 656. The OIC remains pending until an authorized IRS employee accepts, rejects, returns, or acknowledges withdrawal of the offer in writing. If a taxpayer appeals an OIC that was rejected, the IRS will continue to treat the OIC as pending until the Appeals Office accepts or rejects the OIC in writing.

Taxpayers Must File and Pay Taxes — In order to avoid defaulting an OIC once it is accepted by the IRS, taxpayers must remain in compliance in the filing and payment of all required taxes for a period of five years, or until the offered amount is paid in full, whichever is longer. Failure to comply with these conditions will result in the default of the OIC and the reinstatement of the tax liability.

Federal Tax Liens Are Not Released — If there is a Notice of Federal Tax Lien on record prior to the OIC being submitted, the lien is not released until the terms of the offer in compromise are satisfied, or until the liability is paid, whichever comes first. The IRS generally files a Notice of Federal Tax Lien to protect the Government's interest on deferred payment offers. This tax lien will be released when the payment terms of the offer agreement have been satisfied.

Effect of the Offer on the Taxpayer's Refund — The IRS will keep any refund, including interest due to the taxpayer because of overpayment of any tax or other liability, for tax periods extending through the calendar year that the IRS accepts the offer. The taxpayer may not designate an overpayment ordinarily subject to refund, to which the IRS is entitled, to be applied to estimated tax payments for the following year. This condition does not apply if the offer is based on **doubt as to liability**.

Effect of the Offer on Installment Agreements and Levies — The IRS will keep all payments and credits made, received or applied to the total original tax liability before submission of this offer. The IRS may keep any proceeds from a levy served prior to submission of the offer, but not received at the time the offer is submitted. The taxpayer understands that if they had an installment agreement prior to submitting the offer, he/she must continue to make the payments as agreed while this offer is pending. Installment agreement payments will not be applied against the amount offered.

Public Inspection Files for Accepted Offer in Compromise Files — The law requires IRS to make certain information from accepted Offers in Compromise available for public inspection and review. These public inspection files are located in your local IRS Territory Office. It is important to know that certain information regarding your accepted Offer in Compromise may be publicly known.

Taxpayer Advocate Services — If at anytime you feel that you need help in resolving a tax problem that has not been resolved through normal channels or you are experiencing significant hardship, then you may contact our Taxpayer Advocate Service *(TAS)*. To find more information on TAS or to locate your local TAS office, call the nationwide TAS toll-free number 1–877–777–4778, or visit our website at *www.irs.gov*.

Low Income Taxpayer Clinic *(LITC)* — In addition, each taxpayer has a right to representation but not everyone can afford representation. The Low Income Taxpayer Clinic *(LITC)* was developed to represent low income taxpayers before the IRS for free or for a minimal charge. You can learn about LITC by going to our website at *www.irs.gov* and click on Taxpayer Advocate Services, or you can call the nationwide TAS toll-free number 1–877–777–4778.

Terms and Definitions

An understanding of the following terms and conditions will help you to prepare offers based upon **doubt as to collectibility or effective tax administration**.

Current Value — The amount you could reasonably expect from the sale of an asset today. Provide an accurate valuation of each asset. Determine value from realtors, used car dealers, publications, furniture dealers, or other experts on specific types of assets. Please include a copy of any written estimate with your Collection Information Statement.

Expenses Not Generally Allowed — We typically do not allow you to claim tuition for private schools, public or private college expenses, charitable contributions, voluntary retirement contributions, payments on unsecured debts such as credit card bills, cable television charges and other similar expenses as necessary living expenses. However, we can allow these expenses when you can prove that they are necessary for the health and welfare of you or your family or for the production of income.

Future Income — We generally determine the amount we could collect from your future income by subtracting necessary living expenses from your monthly income over a set number of months. For a cash offer, you must offer what you could pay in monthly payments over forty-eight months *(or the remainder of the ten-year statutory period for collection, whichever is less)*. For a short-term deferred offer, you must offer what you could pay in monthly payments over sixty months *(or the remainder of the statutory period for collection, whichever is less)*. For a deferred payment offer, you must offer what you could pay in monthly payments during the remaining time we could legally receive payments.

Necessary Expenses — The allowable payments you make to support you and your family's health and welfare and/or the production of income. This expense allowance does not apply to business entities. Publication 1854, *How to Prepare a Collection Information Statement (Form 433-A)*, explains the National Standard Expenses and gives the allowable amounts. We derive these amounts from the Bureau of Labor Statistics *(BLS)* Consumer Expenditure Survey. We also use information from the Bureau of the Census to determine local expenses for housing, utilities, and transportation.

Note: If the IRS determines that the facts and circumstances of your situation indicate that using the scheduled allowance of necessary expenses is inadequate, we will allow you an adequate means for providing basic living expenses. However, you must provide documentation that supports a determination that using national and local expense standards leaves you an inadequate means of providing for basic living expenses.

Quick Sale Value (QSV) — The amount you could reasonably expect from the sale of an asset if you sold it quickly, typically in ninety days or less. This amount generally is less than current value, but may be equal to or higher, based on local circumstances.

Realizable Value — The quick sale value amount minus what you owe to a secured creditor. The creditor must have priority over a filed Notice of Federal Tax Lien before we allow a subtraction from the asset's value.

Reasonable Collection Potential (RCP) — The total realizable value of your assets plus your future income. The total is generally your minimum offer amount.

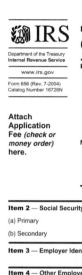

Form 656

Offer in Compromise

Department of the Treasury
Internal Revenue Service

www.irs.gov

Form 656 (Rev. 7-2004)
Catalog Number 16728N

IRS RECEIVED DATE

Item 1 — Taxpayer's Name and Home or Business Street Address

Name

Name

**Attach
Application
Fee (check or
money order)
here.**

Street Address

City   State   ZIP Code

Mailing Address (if different from above)

Street Address

City   State   ZIP Code

DATE RETURNED

Item 2 — Social Security Numbers

(a) Primary

(b) Secondary

Item 3 — Employer Identification Number (included in offer)

Item 4 — Other Employer Identification Numbers (not included in offer) _____

Item 5 — To: Commissioner of Internal Revenue Service

I/We (includes all types of taxpayers) submit this offer to compromise the tax liabilities plus any interest, penalties, additions to tax, and additional amounts required by law (tax liability) for the tax type and period marked below: (Please mark an "X" in the box for the correct description and fill-in the correct tax period(s), adding additional periods if needed).

❏ **1040/1120 Income Tax** — Year(s) _____

❏ **941 Employer's Quarterly Federal Tax Return** — Quarterly period(s) _____

❏ **940 Employer's Annual Federal Unemployment (FUTA) Tax Return** — Year(s) _____

❏ **Trust Fund Recovery Penalty** as a responsible person of (enter corporation name) _____

for failure to pay withholding and Federal Insurance Contributions Act Taxes (Social Security taxes), for period(s) ending _____

❏ **Other Federal Tax(es)** [specify type(s) and period(s)] _____

Note: If you need more space, use another sheet entitled "Attachment to Form 656 Dated _____ ." Sign and date the attachment following the listing of the tax periods.

Item 6 — I/We submit this offer for the reason(s) checked below:

❏ **Doubt as to Liability** — "I do not believe I owe this tax." You must include a detailed explanation of the reason(s) why you believe you do not owe the tax in Item 9.

❏ **Doubt as to Collectibility** — "I have insufficient assets and income to pay the full amount." You must include a complete Collection Information Statement, Form 433-A and/or Form 433-B.

❏ **Effective Tax Administration** — "I owe this amount and have sufficient assets to pay the full amount, but due to my exceptional circumstances, requiring full payment would cause an economic hardship or would be unfair and inequitable." You must include a complete Collection Information Statement, Form 433-A and/or Form 433B **and complete Item 9.**

Item 7

I/We offer to pay $ _____ **(must be more than zero).** Complete item 10 to explain where you will obtain the funds to make this offer.

Check *only* one of the following:

❏ **Cash Offer (Offered amount will be paid in 90 days or less.)**

Balance to be paid in: ❏ 10, ❏ 30, ❏ 60, or ❏ 90 days from written notice of acceptance of the offer.

❏ **Short-Term Deferred Payment Offer (Offered amount paid in MORE than 90 days but within 24 months from written notice of acceptance of the offer.)**

$ _____ within _____ days (not more than 90 — See Instructions Section, **Determine Your Payment Terms**) from written notice of acceptance of the offer; and/or

beginning in the _____ month after written notice of acceptance of the offer $ _____ on the _____ day of each month for a total of _____ months. (Cannot extend more than 24 months from written notice of acceptance of the offer.)

❏ **Deferred Payment Offer (Offered amount will be paid over the remaining life of the collection statute.)**

$ _____ within _____ days (not more than 90 — See Instructions Section, **Determine Your Payment Terms**) from written notice of acceptance of the offer; and

beginning in the first month after written notice of acceptance of the offer $ _____ on the _____ day of each month for a total of _____ months.

Item 8 — By submitting this offer, I/we have read, understand and agree to the following conditions:

(a) I/We voluntarily submit all payments made on this offer.

(b) The IRS will apply payments made under the terms of this offer in the best interest of the government.

(c) If the IRS rejects or returns the offer or I/we withdraw the offer, the IRS will return any amount paid with the offer. However, I/we understand the application fee will be kept by the IRS. If I/we agree in writing, IRS will apply the amount paid with the offer to the amount owed. If I/we agree to apply the payment, the date the IRS received the offer remittance will be considered the date of payment. I/We understand that the IRS will not pay interest on any amount I/we submit with the offer.

(d) I/We will comply with all provisions of the Internal Revenue Code relating to filing my/our returns and paying my/our required taxes for 5 years or until the offered amount is paid in full, whichever is longer. In the case of a jointly submitted offer to compromise joint tax liabilities, I/we understand that default with respect to the compliance provisions described in this paragraph by one party to this agreement will not result in the default of the entire agreement. The default provisions described in Item 8(n) of this agreement will be applied only to the party failing to comply with the requirements of this paragraph. This provision does not apply to offers based on Doubt as to Liability.

(e) I/We waive and agree to the suspension of any statutory periods of limitation (time limits provided for by law) for the IRS assessment or collection of the tax liability for the periods identified in Item 5. I/We understand that I/we have the right not to waive these statutory periods or to limit the waiver to a certain length or to certain issues. I/We understand, however, that the IRS may not consider this offer if I/we refuse to waive the statutory periods for assessment or if we provide only a limited waiver. I/We understand that the statute of limitations for collection will be suspended during the period an offer is considered pending by the IRS *(paragraph 8(m) defines pending)*. The amount of any Federal tax due for the periods described in Item 5 may be assessed at any time prior to the acceptance of this offer or within one year of the rejection of this offer.

(f) The IRS will keep all payments and credits made, received or applied to the total original tax liability before submission of this offer. The IRS may keep any proceeds from a levy served prior to submission of the offer, but not received at the time the offer is submitted. If I/we have an installment agreement prior to submitting the offer, I/we must continue to make the payments as agreed while this offer is pending. Installment agreement payments will not be applied against the amount offered.

(g) As additional consideration beyond the amount of my/our offer, the IRS will keep any refund, including interest, due to me/us because of overpayment of any tax or other liability, for tax periods extending through the calendar year that the IRS accepts the offer. I/We may not designate an overpayment ordinarily subject to refund, to which the IRS is entitled, to be applied to estimated tax payments for the following year. This condition does not apply if the offer is based on Doubt as to Liability.

(h) I/We will return to the IRS any refund identified in (g) received after submission of this offer. This condition does not apply to offers based on Doubt as to Liability.

(i) The IRS cannot collect more than the full amount of the tax liability under this offer.

(j) I/We understand that I/we remain responsible for the full amount of the tax liability, unless and until the IRS accepts the offer in writing and I/we have met all the terms and conditions of the offer. The IRS will not remove the original amount of the tax liability from its records until I/we have met all the terms of the offer.

(k) I/We understand that the tax I/we offer to compromise is and will remain a tax liability until I/we meet all the terms and conditions of this offer. If I/we file bankruptcy before the terms and conditions of this offer are completed, any claim the IRS files in the bankruptcy proceedings will be a tax claim.

(l) Once the IRS accepts the offer in writing, I/we have no right to contest, in court or otherwise, the amount of the tax liability.

(m) The offer is pending starting with the date an authorized IRS official signs this form. The offer remains pending until an authorized IRS official accepts, rejects, returns or acknowledges withdrawal of the offer in writing. If I/we appeal an IRS rejection decision on the offer, the IRS will continue to treat the offer as pending until the Appeals Office accepts or rejects the offer in writing. If I/we don't file a protest within 30 days of the date the IRS notifies me/us of the right to protest the decision, I/we waive the right to a hearing before the Appeals Office about the offer in compromise.

(n) If I/we fail to meet any of the terms and conditions of the offer and the offer defaults, then the IRS may:

- immediately file suit to collect the entire unpaid balance of the offer

- immediately file suit to collect an amount equal to the original amount of the tax liability as liquidating damages, minus any payment already received under the terms of this offer

- disregard the amount of the offer and apply all amounts already paid under the offer against the original amount of the tax liability

- file suit or levy to collect the original amount of the tax liability, without further notice of any kind.

The IRS will continue to add interest, as Section 6601 of the Internal Revenue Code requires, on the amount the IRS determines is due after default. The IRS will add interest from the date the offer is defaulted until I/we completely satisfy the amount owed.

(o) The IRS generally files a Notice of Federal Tax Lien to protect the Government's interest on deferred payment offers. Also, the IRS may file a Notice of Federal Tax Lien during the offer investigation. This tax lien will be released when the payment terms of the offer agreement have been satisfied.

(p) **I/We understand that the IRS employees may contact third parties in order to respond to this request and I/we authorize the IRS to make such contacts. Further, by authorizing the Internal Revenue Service to contact third parties, I/we understand that I will not receive notice, pursuant to section 7602(c) of the Internal Revenue Code, of third parties contacted in connection with this request.**

(q) If doubt as to collectibility and/or effective tax administration are checked in Item 6 above, I/we are offering to compromise all the tax liabilities assessed against me/us as of the date of this offer and under the taxpayer identification numbers listed in Items 2 and/or 3 above. I/We authorize the IRS to amend Item 5, above, to include any assessed liabilities we failed to list on Form 656.

Item 9 — Explanation of Circumstances

I am requesting an offer in compromise for the reason(s) listed below:

*Note: If you are requesting compromise based on doubt as to liability, explain why you don't believe you owe the tax.
If you believe you have special circumstances affecting your ability to fully pay the amount due, explain your situation.
You may attach additional sheets if necessary. Please include your name and SSN or EIN on all additional sheets or
supporting documentation.*

_____

_____

_____

_____

_____

_____

Item 10 — Source of Funds

I / We shall obtain the funds to make this offer from the following source(s):

_____

_____

Item 11 — Mandatory Signature(s)

If I / We submit this offer on a substitute form, I / we affirm that this
form is a verbatim duplicate of the official Form 656, and I/we
agree to be bound by all the terms and conditions set forth in the
official Form 656.

Under penalties of perjury, I declare that I have examined this
offer, including accompanying schedules and statements, and
to the best of my knowledge and belief, it is true, correct and
complete.

_____
11(a) Signature of Taxpayer

_____
Date

_____
11(b) Signature of Taxpayer

_____
Date

For Official Use Only

I accept the waiver of the statutory period of limitations on assessment
for the Internal Revenue Service, as described in Item 8(e).

_____
Signature of Authorized Internal Revenue Service Official

_____
Title

_____
Date

Item 12 — If this application was prepared by someone other than the tapayer, please fill in that person's name and address below.

Name: _____

Address: _____
(if known)

Item 13 **Paid Preparer's Use Only**	Preparer's ▶ signature		Date	Check if self-employed ☐	Preparer's CAF no. or PTIN
	Firm's name (or yours if self-employed), address, and ZIP code ▶			EIN	
				Phone no. ( )	

Item 14 **Third Party Designee**	Do you want to allow another person to discuss this offer with the IRS?		☐ Yes. Complete the following.		☐ No
	Designee's name ▶		Phone ▶ ( ) no.		

IRS

Department of the Treasury
Internal Revenue Service

www.irs.gov

Form 433-A (Rev. 5-2001)
Catalog Number 20312N

Collection Information Statement for Wage Earners and Self-Employed Individuals

Complete all entry spaces with the most current data available.

Important! Write "N/A" (not applicable) in spaces that do not apply. We may require additional information to support "N/A" entries.

Failure to complete all entry spaces may result in rejection or significant delay in the resolution of your account.

Section 1 **Personal Information**	1. Full Name(s) _____	1a. Home Telephone (___) _____	Best Time To Call: ___ am ___ pm (Enter Hour)

Section 1
Personal Information

1. Full Name(s) _____
Street Address _____
City _____ State _____ Zip _____
County of Residence _____
How long at this address? _____

1a. Home
Telephone (____) _____
Best Time To Call:
____ am ____ pm
(Enter Hour)

2. Marital Status:
☐ Married   ☐ Separated
☐ Unmarried (single, divorced, widowed)

3. Your Social Security No.(SSN) _____ | _____
4. Spouse's Social Security No. _____ | _____

3a. Your Date of Birth (mm/dd/yyyy) _____
4a. Spouse's Date of Birth (mm/dd/yyyy) _____

5. ☐ Own Home   ☐ Rent   ☐ Other (specify, i.e. share rent, live with relative) _____

6. List the dependents you can claim on your tax return: (Attach sheet if more space is needed.)

First Name	Relationship	Age	Does this person live with you?	First Name	Relationship	Age	Does this person live with you?
			☐ No ☐ Yes				☐ No ☐ Yes
			☐ No ☐ Yes				☐ No ☐ Yes

☐ Check this box when all spaces in Sect. 1 are filled in.

Section 2
Your Business Information

☐ Check this box when all spaces in Sect. 2 are filled in and attachments provided.

7. Are you or your spouse self-employed or operate a business? (Check "Yes" if either applies)

☐ No   ☐ Yes   If yes, provide the following information:

7a. Name of Business _____
7b. Street Address _____
City _____ State _____ Zip _____

7c. Employer Identification No., if available : _____
7d. Do you have employees?   ☐ No   ☐ Yes
7e. Do you have accounts/notes receivable?   ☐ No   ☐ Yes

If yes, please complete Section 8 on page 5.

ATTACHMENTS REQUIRED: Please include proof of self-employment income for the **prior 3 months** (e.g., invoices, commissions, sales records, income statement).

Section 3
Employment Information

☐ Check this box when all spaces in Sect. 3 are filled in and attachments provided.

8. Your Employer _____
Street Address _____
City _____ State _____ Zip _____
Work telephone no. (_____) _____
May we contact you at work?   ☐ No   ☐ Yes
8a. How long with this employer? _____
8b. Occupation _____

9. Spouse's Employer _____
Street Address _____
City _____ State _____ Zip _____
Work telephone no. (_____) _____
May we contact you at work?   ☐ No   ☐ Yes
9a. How long with this employer? _____
9b. Occupation _____

ATTACHMENTS REQUIRED: Please provide proof of gross earnings and deductions for the past 3 months from each employer (e.g., pay stubs, earnings statements). If year-to-date information is available, send only 1 such statement as long as a **minimum of 3 months** is represented.

Section 4
Other Income Information

☐ Check this box when all spaces in Sect. 4 are filled in and attachments provided.

10. Do you receive income from sources other than your own business or your employer? (Check all that apply.)

☐ Pension   ☐ Social Security   ☐ Other (specify, i.e. child support, alimony, rental) _____

ATTACHMENTS REQUIRED: Please provide proof of pension/social security/other income for the past 3 months from each payor, including any statements showing deductions. If year-to-date information is available, send only 1 such statement as long as a **minimum of 3 months** is represented.

Collection Information Statement for Wage Earners and Self-Employed Individuals   **Form 433-A**

Name_____ SSN_____

Section 5	**11. CHECKING ACCOUNTS.** List all checking accounts. (If you need additional space, attach a separate sheet.)

Banking, Investment, Cash, Credit, and Life Insurance Information

	Type of Account	Full Name of Bank, Savings & Loan, Credit Union or Financial Institution	Bank Routing No.	Bank Account No.	Current Account Balance
11a.	Checking	Name _____	_____	_____	$ _____
		Street Address _____			
		City/State/Zip _____			
11b.	Checking	Name _____	_____	_____	$ _____
		Street Address _____			
		City/State/Zip _____	**11c. Total Checking Account Balances**		$

Complete all entry spaces with the most current data available.

12. OTHER ACCOUNTS. List all acounts, including brokerage, savings, and money market, not listed on line 11.

	Type of Account	Full Name of Bank, Savings & Loan, Credit Union or Financial Institution	Bank Routing No.	Bank Account No.	Current Account Balance
12a.	_____	Name _____	_____	_____	$ _____
		Street Address _____			
		City/State/Zip _____			
12b.	_____	Name _____	_____	_____	$ _____
		Street Address _____			
		City/State/Zip _____	**12c. Total Other Account Balances**		$

ATTACHMENTS REQUIRED: Please include your current bank statements (checking, savings, money market, and brokerage accounts) for the past three months for all accounts.

13. INVESTMENTS. List all investment assets below. Include stocks, bonds, mutual funds, stock options, certificates of deposits, and retirement assets such as IRAs, Keogh, and 401(k) plans. (If you need additional space, attach a separate sheet.)

	Name of Company	Number of Shares / Units	¤ Current Value	Loan Amount	Used as collateral on loan?
13a.	_____	_____	$ _____	$ _____	☐ No ☐ Yes
13b.	_____	_____	_____	_____	☐ No ☐ Yes
13c.	_____	_____	_____	_____	☐ No ☐ Yes
		13d. Total Investments	$		

¤ Current Value: Indicate the amount you could sell the asset for today.

14. CASH ON HAND. Include any money that you have that is not in the bank.

14a. Total Cash on Hand $

15. AVAILABLE CREDIT. List all lines of credit, including credit cards.

	Full Name of Credit Institution	Credit Limit	Amount Owed	Available Credit
15a.	Name_____	_____	_____	$ _____
	Street Address_____			
	City/State/Zip_____			
15b.	Name_____	_____	_____	$ _____
	Street Address_____			
	City/State/Zip_____	**15c. Total Credit Available**		$

Section 5 continued on page 3 →
(Rev. 5-2001)

Collection Information Statement for Wage Earners and Self-Employed Individuals　　　**Form 433-A**

Name _____　SSN_____

| **Section 5**
continued | **16. LIFE INSURANCE.** Do you have life insurance with a cash value?　☐ No ☐ Yes
(Term Life insurance does not have a cash value.)
If yes:
16a. Name of Insurance Company _____
16b. Policy Number(s) _____
16c. Owner of Policy _____
16d. Current Cash Value $ _____　　**16e.** Outstanding Loan Balance $_____ |
| ☐ Check this box
when all spaces in
Sect. 5 are filled in
and attachments
provided. | Subtract "Outstanding Loan Balance" line 16e from "Current Cash Value" line 16d = 16f　$_____

ATTACHMENTS REQUIRED: Please include a statement from the life insurance companies that
includes type and cash/loan value amounts. If currently borrowed against, include loan amount
and date of loan. |

| **Section 6**
Other
Information | **17. OTHER INFORMATION.** Respond to the following questions related to your financial condition: (Attach sheet if you need
more space.)

17a. Are there any garnishments against your wages?　☐ No ☐ Yes
If yes, who is the creditor?_____　Date creditor obtained judgement _____　Amount of debt $_____
17b. Are there any judgments against you?　☐ No ☐ Yes
If yes, who is the creditor?_____　Date creditor obtained judgement _____　Amount of debt $_____
17c. Are you a party in a lawsuit?　☐ No ☐ Yes
If yes, amount of suit $_____　Possible completion date _____　Subject matter of suit _____
17d. Did you ever file bankruptcy?　☐ No ☐ Yes
If yes, date filed _____　Date discharged _____
17e. In the past 10 years did you transfer any
assets out of your name for less than
their actual value?　☐ No ☐ Yes
If yes, what asset? _____　Value of asset at time of transfer $_____
When was it transferred?_____　To whom was it transferred? _____
17f. Do you anticipate any increase in household
income in the next two years?　☐ No ☐ Yes
If yes, why will the income increase? _____　(Attach sheet if you need more space.)
How much will it increase?　$ _____
17g. Are you a beneficiary of a trust or an estate?　☐ No ☐ Yes
If yes, name of the trust or estate_____　Anticipated amount to be received $_____
When will the amount be received? _____ |
| ☐ Check this box
when all spaces in
Sect. 6 are filled in. | **17h.** Are you a participant in a profit sharing plan?　☐ No ☐ Yes
If yes, name of plan _____　Value in plan $ _____ |

| **Section 7**
Assets and
Liabilities | **18. PURCHASED AUTOMOBILES, TRUCKS AND OTHER LICENSED ASSETS.** Include boats, RV's, motorcycles, trailers, etc.
(If you need additional space, attach a separate sheet.) |

	Description (Year, Make, Model, Mileage)	¤ Current Value	Current Loan Balance	Name of Lender	Purchase Date	Amount of Monthly Payment
¤ Current **Value:** Indicate the amount you could sell the asset for today.	**18a.** Year Make/Model Mileage	$	$			$
	18b. Year Make/Model Mileage	$	$			$
	18c. Year Make/Model Mileage	$	$			$

Section 7 continued on page 4 →
(Rev. 5-2001)

Collection Information Statement for Wage Earners and Self-Employed Individuals　　　**Form 433-A**

Name_____　SSN_____

Section 7 continued	19.	**LEASED AUTOMOBILES, TRUCKS AND OTHER LICENSED ASSETS.** Include boats, RV's, motorcycles, trailers, etc. (If you need additional space, attach a separate sheet.)				

		Description (Year, Make, Model)	Lease Balance	Name and Address of Lessor	Lease Date	Amount of Monthly Payment
	19a.	Year _____ Make/Model _____	$			$
	19b.	Year _____ Make/Model _____	$			$

ATTACHMENTS REQUIRED: Please include your current statement from lender with monthly car payment amount and current balance of the loan for each vehicle purchased or leased.

20. **REAL ESTATE.** List all real estate you own. (If you need additional space, attach a separate sheet.)

	Street Address, City, State, Zip, and County	Date Purchased	Purchase Price	☐ Current Value	Loan Balance	Name of Lender or Lien Holder	Amount of Monthly Payment	✸ Date of Final Payment
20a.			$	$	$		$	
20b.			$	$	$		$	

☐ **Current Value:** Indicate the amount you could sell the asset for today.

✸ **Date of Final Payment:** Enter the date the loan or lease will be fully paid.

ATTACHMENTS REQUIRED: Please include your current statement from lender with monthly payment amount and current balance for each piece of real estate owned.

21. **PERSONAL ASSETS.** List all Personal assets below. (If you need additional space, attach separate sheet.) *Furniture/Personal Effects* includes the total current market value of your household such as furniture and appliances. *Other Personal Assets* includes all artwork, jewelry, collections (coin/gun, etc.), antiques or other assets.

	Description	☐ Current Value	Loan Balance	Name of Lender	Amount of Monthly Payment	✸ Date of Final Payment
21a.	Furniture/Personal Effects	$	$		$	
	Other: (List below)					
21b.	Artwork	$	$		$	
21c.	Jewelry					
21d.						
21e.						

22. **BUSINESS ASSETS.** List all business assets and encumbrances below, include Uniform Commercial Code (UCC) filings. (If you need additional space, attach a separate sheet.) *Tools used in Trade or Business* includes the basic tools or books used to conduct your business, excluding automobiles. *Other Business Assets* includes any other machinery, equipment, inventory or other assets.

	Description	☐ Current Value	Loan Balance	Name of Lender	Amount of Monthly Payment	✸ Date of Final Payment
22a.	Tools used in Trade/Business	$	$		$	
	Other: (List below)					
22b.	Machinery	$	$		$	
22c.	Equipment					
22d.						
22e.						

☐ Check this box when all spaces in Sect. 7 are filled in and attachments provided.

Collection Information Statement for Wage Earners and Self-Employed Individuals　　　　**Form 433-A**

Name_____　SSN_____

Section 8 Accounts/ Notes Receivable	**23. ACCOUNTS/NOTES RECEIVABLE.** List all accounts separately, including contracts awarded, but not started. (If you need additional space, attach a separate sheet.)

	Description	Amount Due	Date Due	Age of Account

Use only if needed.

☐ *Check this box if Section 8 not needed.*

23a. Name _____　$_____　_____
　　　Street Address _____
　　　City/State/Zip_____
　☐ 0 - 30 days ☐ 30 - 60 days ☐ 60 - 90 days ☐ 90+ days

23b. Name _____　$_____　_____
　　　Street Address _____
　　　City/State/Zip_____
　☐ 0 - 30 days ☐ 30 - 60 days ☐ 60 - 90 days ☐ 90+ days

23c. Name _____　$_____
　　　Street Address _____
　　　City/State/Zip_____
　☐ 0 - 30 days ☐ 30 - 60 days ☐ 60 - 90 days ☐ 90+ days

23d. Name _____　$_____
　　　Street Address _____
　　　City/State/Zip_____
　☐ 0 - 30 days ☐ 30 - 60 days ☐ 60 - 90 days ☐ 90+ days

23e. Name _____　$_____　_____
　　　Street Address _____
　　　City/State/Zip_____
　☐ 0 - 30 days ☐ 30 - 60 days ☐ 60 - 90 days ☐ 90+ days

23f. Name _____　$_____
　　　Street Address _____
　　　City/State/Zip_____
　☐ 0 - 30 days ☐ 30 - 60 days ☐ 60 - 90 days ☐ 90+ days

23g. Name _____　$_____
　　　Street Address _____
　　　City/State/Zip_____
　☐ 0 - 30 days ☐ 30 - 60 days ☐ 60 - 90 days ☐ 90+ days

23h. Name _____　$_____
　　　Street Address _____
　　　City/State/Zip_____
　☐ 0 - 30 days ☐ 30 - 60 days ☐ 60 - 90 days ☐ 90+ days

23i. Name _____　$_____
　　　Street Address _____
　　　City/State/Zip_____
　☐ 0 - 30 days ☐ 30 - 60 days ☐ 60 - 90 days ☐ 90+ days

23j. Name _____　$_____　_____
　　　Street Address _____
　　　City/State/Zip_____
　☐ 0 - 30 days ☐ 30 - 60 days ☐ 60 - 90 days ☐ 90+ days

23k. Name _____　$_____
　　　Street Address _____
　　　City/State/Zip_____
　☐ 0 - 30 days ☐ 30 - 60 days ☐ 60 - 90 days ☐ 90+ days

23l. Name _____　$_____
　　　Street Address _____
　　　City/State/Zip_____
　☐ 0 - 30 days ☐ 30 - 60 days ☐ 60 - 90 days ☐ 90+ days

☐ *Check this box when all spaces in Sect. 8 are filled in.*

Add "Amount Due" from lines 23a through 23l = 23m $_____

Collection Information Statement for Wage Earners and Self-Employed Individuals   **Form 433-A**

Name _____   SSN _____

Section 9	Total Income			Total Living Expenses		
Monthly Income and Expense Analysis	Source	Gross Monthly		Expense Items [4]	Actual Monthly	
	24. Wages (Yourself)[1]	$		35. Food, Clothing and Misc.[5]	$	
	25. Wages (Spouse)[1]			36. Housing and Utilities[6]		
	26. Interest - Dividends			37. Transportation[7]		
	27. Net Income from Business[2]			38. Health Care		
If only one spouse has a tax liability, but both have income, list the total household income and expenses.	28. Net Rental Income[3]			39. Taxes (Income and FICA)		
	29. Pension/Social Security (Yourself)			40. Court ordered payments		
	30. Pension/Social Security (Spouse)			41. Child/dependent care		
	31. Child Support			42. Life insurance		
	32. Alimony			43. Other secured debt		
	33. Other			44. Other expenses		
	34. Total Income	$		45. Total Living Expenses	$	

[1] **Wages, salaries, pensions, and social security:** Enter your gross monthly wages and/or salaries. Do not deduct withholding or allotments you elect to take out of your pay, such as insurance payments, credit union deductions, car payments etc.
To calculate your gross monthly wages and/or salaries:
   If paid weekly - multiply weekly gross wages by 4.3. Example: $425.89 x 4.3 = $1,831.33
   If paid bi-weekly (every 2 weeks) - multiply bi-weekly gross wages by 2.17. Example: $972.45 x 2.17 = $2,110.22
   If paid semi-monthly (twice each month) - multiply semi-monthly gross wages by 2. Example: $856.23 x 2 = $1,712.46

[2] **Net Income from Business:** Enter your monthly net business income. This is the amount you earn after you pay ordinary and necessary monthly business expenses. This figure should relate to the yearly net profit from your Form 1040 Schedule C. If it is more or less than the previous year, you should attach an explanation. If your net business income is a loss, enter "0". Do not enter a negative number.

[3] **Net Rental Income:** Enter your monthly net rental income. This is the amount you earn after you pay ordinary and necessary monthly rental expenses. If your net rental income is a loss, enter "0". Do not enter a negative number.

[4] **Expenses not generally allowed:** We generally do not allow you to claim tuition for private schools, public or private college expenses, charitable contributions, voluntary retirement contributions, payments on unsecured debts such as credit card bills, cable television and other similar expenses. However, we may allow these expenses, if you can prove that they are necessary for the health and welfare of you or your family or for the production of income.

[5] **Food, Clothing and Misc.:** Total of clothing, food, housekeeping supplies and personal care products for one month.

[6] **Housing and Utilities:** For your principal residence: Total of rent or mortgage payment. Add the average monthly expenses for the following: property taxes, home owner's or renter's insurance, maintenance, dues, fees, and utilities. Utilities include gas, electricity, water, fuel, oil, other fuels, trash collection and telephone.

[7] **Transportation:** Total of lease or purchase payments, vehicle insurance, registration fees, normal maintenance, fuel, public transportation, parking and tolls for one month.

ATTACHMENTS REQUIRED: Please include:

- A copy of your last Form 1040 with all Schedules.

- Proof of all current expenses that you paid for the past 3 months, including utilities, rent, insurance, property taxes, etc.

- Proof of all non-business transportation expenses (e.g., car payments, lease payments, fuel, oil, insurance, parking, registration).

- Proof of payments for health care, including health insurance premiums, co-payments, and other out-of-pocket expenses, for the past 3 months.

- Copies of any court order requiring payment and proof of such payments (e.g., cancelled checks, money orders, earning statements showing such deductions) for the past 3 months.

☐ Check this box when all spaces in Sect. 9 are filled in and attachments provided.

☐ Check this box when all spaces in all sections are filled in and all attachments provided.

⚠ CAUTION   *Failure to complete all entry spaces may result in rejection or significant delay in the resolution of your account.*

Certification: *Under penalties of perjury, I declare that to the best of my knowledge and belief this statement of assets, liabilities, and other information is true, correct and complete.*

Your Signature _____   Spouse's Signature _____   Date _____

(Rev. 5-2001)

IRS   ## Collection Information Statement for Businesses

Department of the Treasury
Internal Revenue Service

www.irs.gov

Form 433-B (Rev. 5-2001)
Catalog Number 16649P

Complete all entry spaces with the most current data available.

Important! Write "N/A" (not applicable) in spaces that do not apply. We may require additional information to support "N/A" entries.

Failure to complete all entry spaces may result in rejection or significant delay in the resolution of your account.

Section 1

Business Information

☐ Check this box when all spaces in Sect. 1 are filled in.

1a. Business Name _____
Business Street Address _____
_____
City_____ State_____ Zip_____
County _____
1b. Business Telephone (___) _____
2a. Employer Identification No. (EIN) _____
2b. Type of Entity (Check appropriate box below)
☐ Partnership ☐ Corporation ☐ Other _____
2c. Type of Business _____

3a. Contact Name _____
3b. Contact's Business Telephone (___) _____
Extension _____
Best Time To Call _____ am _____ pm (Enter Hour)
3c. Contact's Home Telephone (___) _____
Best Time To Call _____ am _____ pm (Enter Hour)
3d. Contact's Other Telephone (___) _____
Telephone Type (i.e. fax, cellular, pager) _____
3e. Contact's E-mail Address _____

Section 2

Business Personnel and Contacts

☐ Check this box when all spaces in Sect. 2 are filled in.

4. PERSON RESPONSIBLE FOR DEPOSITING PAYROLL TAXES

4a. Full Name_____ Title _____
Home Street Address _____
City_____ State_____ Zip_____

Social Security Number _____ | _____ |
Home Telephone (___) _____
Ownership Percentage & Shares or Interest _____

5. PARTNERS, OFFICERS, MAJOR SHAREHOLDERS, ETC.

5a. Full Name_____ Title_____
Home Street Address _____
City_____ State_____ Zip_____

Social Security Number _____ | _____ |
Home Telephone (___) _____
Ownership Percentage & Shares or Interest _____

5b. Full Name_____ Title_____
Home Street Address _____
City_____ State_____ Zip_____

Social Security Number _____ | _____ |
Home Telephone (___) _____
Ownership Percentage & Shares or Interest _____

5c. Full Name_____ Title_____
Home Street Address _____
City_____ State_____ Zip_____

Social Security Number _____ | _____ |
Home Telephone (___) _____
Ownership Percentage & Shares or Interest _____

5d. Full Name_____ Title_____
Home Street Address _____
City_____ State_____ Zip_____

Social Security Number _____ | _____ |
Home Telephone (___) _____
Ownership Percentage & Shares or Interest _____

Section 3

Accounts/ Notes Receivable

See page 6 for additional space, if needed.

☐ Check this box when all spaces in Sect. 3 are filled in.

6. ACCOUNTS/NOTES RECEIVABLE. List all contracts separately, including contracts awarded, but not started.

Description	Amount Due	Date Due	Age of Account
6a. Name _____	$ _____	_____	☐ 0 - 30 days
Street Address _____			☐ 30 - 60 days
City/State/Zip _____			☐ 60 - 90 days
			☐ 90+ days
6b. Name _____	$ _____	_____	☐ 0 - 30 days
Street Address _____			☐ 30 - 60 days
City/State/Zip _____			☐ 60 - 90 days
			☐ 90+ days

6a + 6b = 6c   6c $ _____

Amount from Page 6 +   6p _____

6q. Total Accounts/ Notes Receivable =   6c + 6p = 6q $ _____

Collection Information Statement for Businesses   **Form 433-B**

Business Name _____   EIN _____

Section 4	7.	**OTHER FINANCIAL INFORMATION.** Respond to the following business financial questions.

Section 4
Other
Financial
Information

7a. Does this business have other business relationships (e.g. subsidiary or parent, corporation, partnership, etc.)? .... ☐ No ☐ Yes
If yes, list related EIN _____   Additional EIN _____

7b. Does anyone (e.g. officer, stockholder, partner or employees) have an outstanding loan borrowed from the business? .... ☐ No ☐ Yes
If yes, amount of loan $ _____ Date of loan _____ Current balance $_____

7c. Are there any judgments or liens against your business? .... ☐ No ☐ Yes
If yes, who is the creditor?_____ Date creditor obtained judgment/lien _____ Amount of debt $ _____

7d. Is your business a party in a lawsuit? .... ☐ No ☐ Yes
If yes, amount of suit $ _____ Possible completion date _____ Subject matter of suit_____

7e. Has your business ever filed bankruptcy? .... ☐ No ☐ Yes
If yes, date filed _____ Date discharged _____ Petition No._____

7f. In the past 10 years have you transferred any assets from your business name for less than their actual value? .... ☐ No ☐ Yes
If yes, what asset? _____ Value of asset at time of transfer $_____
When was it transferred? _____ To whom or where was it transferred?_____

7g. Do you anticipate any increase in business income (e.g. contracts bid but not yet awarded)? .... ☐ No ☐ Yes
If yes, why will the income increase? _____ ..... (Attach sheet if you need additional space.)
How much will it increase? _____ When will the business income increase?_____

☐ Check this box
when all spaces in
Sect. 4 are filled in.

7h. Is your business a beneficiary of a trust, an estate or a life insurance policy? .... ☐ No ☐ Yes
If yes, name of the trust, estate or policy? _____ Anticipated amount to be received?_____
When will the amount be received?_____

Section 5
Business
Assets

⋈ Current
Value:
Indicate the
amount you
could sell the
asset for today.

8. **PURCHASED AUTOMOBILES, TRUCKS AND OTHER LICENSED ASSETS.** Include boats, RV's, motorcycles, trailers, etc.
(If you need additional space, attach a separate sheet.)

Description (Year, Make, Model, Mileage)	⋈ Current Value	Loan Balance	Name of Lender	Purchase Date	Amount of Monthly Payment
8a. Year					
Make/Model					
Mileage	$	$			$
8b. Year					
Make/Model					
Mileage	$	$			$
8c. Year					
Make/Model					
Mileage	$	$			$

9. **LEASED AUTOMOBILES, TRUCKS AND OTHER LICENSED ASSETS.** Include boats, RV's, motorcycles, trailers, etc.
(If you need additional space, attach a separate sheet.)

Description (Year, Make, Model)	Lease Balance	Name of Lessor	Lease Date	Amount of Monthly Payment
9a. Year				
Make/Model	$			$
9b. Year				
Make/Model	$			$

ATTACHMENTS REQUIRED: Please include your current statement from lender with monthly
car payment amount and current balance of the loan for each vehicle purchased or leased.

Section 5 continued on page 3 →
(Rev. 5-2001)

Collection Information Statement for Businesses   **Form 433-B**

Business Name _____   EIN _____

Section 5	10. **REAL ESTATE.** List all real estate owned by the business. (If you need additional space, attach a separate sheet.)

Section 5 continued

¤ **Current Value:** Indicate the amount you could sell the asset for today.

✱**Date of Final Payment:** Enter the date the loan or lease will be fully paid.

	Street Address, City, State, Zip, and County	Date Purchased	Purchase Price	¤Current Value	Loan Balance	Name of Lender or Lien Holder	Amount of Monthly Payment	✱Date of Final Payment
10a.			$	$	$		$	
10b.			$	$	$		$	

ATTACHMENTS REQUIRED: Please include your current statement from lender with monthly payment amount and current balance for each piece of real estate owned.

☐ *Check this box if you are attaching a depreciation schedule for machinery/ equipment in lieu of completing line 11.*

11. **BUSINESS ASSETS.** List all business assets and encumbrances below, include Uniform Commercial Code (UCC) filings. (If you need additional space, attach a separate sheet.)   Note: If attaching a depreciation schedule, the attachment must include all of the information requested below.

	Description	¤Current Value	Loan Balance	Name of Lender	Amount of Monthly Payment	✱Date of Final Payment
11a.	Machinery	$	$		$	
	Equipment					
	Merchandise					
	Other Assets: (List below)					
11b.		$	$		$	
11c.						

ATTACHMENTS REQUIRED: Please include your current statement from lender with monthly payment amount and current loan balance for assets listed which have an encumbrance.

☐ Check this box when all spaces in Sect. 5 are filled in and attachments provided.

Section 6

Investment, Banking and Cash Information

12. **INVESTMENTS.** List all investment assets below. Include stocks, bonds, mutual funds, stock options and certificates of deposits.

	Name of Company	Number of Shares / Units	¤Current Value	Loan Amount	Used as collateral on loan?
12a.			$	$	☐ No ☐ Yes
12b.					☐ No ☐ Yes
	12c. **Total Investments**		$		

Section 6 continued on page 4 →
(Rev. 5-2001)

Collection Information Statement for Businesses　　　　　　　　　　　　**Form 433-B**

Business Name _____　EIN _____

Section 6
continued

Complete all entry spaces with the most current data available.

13. BANK ACCOUNTS. List all checking and savings accounts. (If you need additional space, attach a separate sheet.)

	Type of Account	Full Name of Bank, Savings & Loan, Credit Union or Financial Institution	Bank Routing No.	Bank Account No.	Current Account Balance
13a. Checking	Name _____ Street Address _____ City/State/Zip _____		_____	_____	$ _____
13b. Checking	Name _____ Street Address _____ City/State/Zip _____		_____	_____	$ _____
13c. Savings	Name _____ Street Address _____ City/State/Zip _____		_____	_____	$ _____

13d. Total Bank Account Balances $ _____

ATTACHMENTS REQUIRED: Please include your current bank statements (checking and savings) for the past three months for all accounts.

14. OTHER ACCOUNTS. List all accounts including brokerage accounts, money market, additional checking and savings accounts not listed on line #13 and any other accounts not listed in this section.

	Type of Account	Full Name of Bank, Savings & Loan, Credit Union or Financial Institution	Bank Routing No.	Bank Account No.	Current Account Balance
14a. _____	Name _____ Street Address _____ City/State/Zip _____		_____	_____	$ _____
14b. _____	Name _____ Street Address _____ City/State/Zip _____		_____	_____	$ _____

14c. Total Other Account Balances $ _____

ATTACHMENTS REQUIRED: Please include your current bank statements (checking, savings, money market, and brokerage accounts) for the past three months for all accounts.

15. CASH ON HAND. Include any money that you have that is not in the bank.

15a. Total Cash on Hand $ _____

16. AVAILABLE CREDIT. List all lines of credit, including credit cards.

Full Name of Credit Institution	Credit Limit	Amount Owed	Available Credit
16a. Name _____ Street Address _____ City/State/Zip _____	_____	_____	$ _____
16b. Name _____ Street Address _____ City/State/Zip _____			$ _____

☐ Check this box when all spaces in Sect. 6 are filled in and attachments provided.

16c. Total Credit Available $ _____

Collection Information Statement for Businesses   Form 433-B

Business Name _____   EIN _____

Section 7 **Monthly Income and Expenses**	**17.** The following information applies to income and expenses from your most recently filed Form 1120 or Form 1065. Fiscal Year Period _____ to _____ **18.** Accounting Method Used: ☐ Cash ☐ Accrual

Complete all entry spaces with the most current data available.

The information included on lines 19 through 39 should reconcile to your business federal tax return.

Total Income			*Total Expenses*	
Source	**Gross Monthly**		**Expense Items**	**Actual Monthly**
19. Gross Receipts	$		27. Materials Purchased [1]	$
20. Gross Rental Income			28. Inventory Purchased [2]	
21. Interest			29. Gross Wages & Salaries	
22. Dividends			30. Rent	
Other Income (specify in lines 23-25)			31. Supplies [3]	
23.			32. Utilities / Telephone [4]	
24.			33. Vehicle Gasoline / Oil	
25.			34. Repairs & Maintenance	
(Add lines 19 through 25)			35. Insurance	
26. **TOTAL INCOME**	$		36. Current Taxes [5]	
			Other Expenses (include installment payments, specify in lines 37-38)	
			37.	
			38.	
			(Add lines 27 through 38)	
			39. **TOTAL EXPENSES**	$

[1] **Materials Purchased:** Materials are items directly related to the production of a product or service.

[2] **Inventory Purchased:** Goods bought for resale.

[3] **Supplies:** Supplies are items used in your business that are consumed or used up within one year, this could be the cost of books, office supplies, professional instruments, etc.

[4] **Utilities:** Utilities include gas, electricity, water, fuel, oil, other fuels, trash collection and telephone.

[5] **Current Taxes:** Real estate, state and local income tax, excise, franchise, occupational, personal property, sales and the employer's portion of employment taxes.

☐ Check this box when all spaces in Sect. 7 are filled in.

☐ Check this box when all spaces in all sections are filled in and all attachments provided.

⚠ **CAUTION**   *Failure to complete all entry spaces may result in rejection or significant delay in the resolution of your account.*

Certification: Under penalties of perjury, I declare that to the best of my knowledge and belief this statement of assets, liabilities, and other information is true, correct and complete.

_____   _____
Print Name   Title

✍ _____   _____
Your Signature   Date

Collection Information Statement for Businesses   Form 433-B

Business Name _____   EIN _____

Section 3	ACCOUNTS/NOTES RECEIVABLE CONTINUATION PAGE. List all contracts separately, including contracts awarded, but not

Section 3
Accounts/
Notes
Receivable
continued

Use only if needed.

☐ *Check this box if this page is not needed.*

ACCOUNTS/NOTES RECEIVABLE CONTINUATION PAGE. List all contracts separately, including contracts awarded, but not started. (If you need additional space, copy this page and attach to the 433-B package.)

	Description	Amount Due	Date Due	Age of Account
6d.	Name _____	$ _____	_____	☐ 0 - 30 days ☐ 30 - 60 days ☐ 60 - 90 days ☐ 90+ days
	Street Address _____			
	City/State/Zip _____			
6e.	Name _____	$ _____	_____	☐ 0 - 30 days ☐ 30 - 60 days ☐ 60 - 90 days ☐ 90+ days
	Street Address _____			
	City/State/Zip _____			
6f.	Name _____	$ _____	_____	☐ 0 - 30 days ☐ 30 - 60 days ☐ 60 - 90 days ☐ 90+ days
	Street Address _____			
	City/State/Zip _____			
6g.	Name _____	$ _____	_____	☐ 0 - 30 days ☐ 30 - 60 days ☐ 60 - 90 days ☐ 90+ days
	Street Address _____			
	City/State/Zip _____			
6h.	Name _____	$ _____	_____	☐ 0 - 30 days ☐ 30 - 60 days ☐ 60 - 90 days ☐ 90+ days
	Street Address _____			
	City/State/Zip _____			
6i.	Name _____	$ _____	_____	☐ 0 - 30 days ☐ 30 - 60 days ☐ 60 - 90 days ☐ 90+ days
	Street Address _____			
	City/State/Zip _____			
6j.	Name _____	$ _____	_____	☐ 0 - 30 days ☐ 30 - 60 days ☐ 60 - 90 days ☐ 90+ days
	Street Address _____			
	City/State/Zip _____			
6k.	Name _____	$ _____	_____	☐ 0 - 30 days ☐ 30 - 60 days ☐ 60 - 90 days ☐ 90+ days
	Street Address _____			
	City/State/Zip _____			
6l.	Name _____	$ _____	_____	☐ 0 - 30 days ☐ 30 - 60 days ☐ 60 - 90 days ☐ 90+ days
	Street Address _____			
	City/State/Zip _____			
6m.	Name _____	$ _____	_____	☐ 0 - 30 days ☐ 30 - 60 days ☐ 60 - 90 days ☐ 90+ days
	Street Address _____			
	City/State/Zip _____			
6n.	Name _____	$ _____	_____	☐ 0 - 30 days ☐ 30 - 60 days ☐ 60 - 90 days ☐ 90+ days
	Street Address _____			
	City/State/Zip _____			
6o.	Name _____	$ _____	_____	☐ 0 - 30 days ☐ 30 - 60 days ☐ 60 - 90 days ☐ 90+ days
	Street Address _____			
	City/State/Zip _____			

☐ Check this box when all spaces in Sect. 3 are filled in.

Add lines 6d through 6o = 6p $ [   ]   *(Add this amount to amount on line 6c, Section 3, page 1)*

(Rev. 5-2001)

Offer in Compromise *(OIC)* Application Fee Worksheet

Keep this worksheet for your records.
Do not send to IRS.

If your OIC is based solely on Doubt as to Liability, do not submit the fee.

If you answered YES to any of the questions on page 3, **then do not proceed any further.** You are not eligible to have your offer considered at this time.

If you answered NO to all of the questions on page 3, then you may be eligible to have your offer considered and you may proceed completing the worksheet. However, it is important that you use the current version Form 656, *Offer in Compromise*, and Forms 433-A, *Collection Information Statement for Wage Earners and Self-Employed Individuals*, and/or 433-B, *Collection Information Statement for Businesses* that are included in this package.

The application fee does not apply to individuals whose income falls at or below levels based on poverty guidelines established by the U.S. Department of Health and Human Services (HHS) under authority of section 673(2) of the Omnibus Reconciliation Act of 1981 (95 Stat. 357, 511). The exception for taxpayers with incomes below these levels only applies to individuals; it does not apply to other entities such as corporations or partnerships.

If you are an individual, follow the steps below to determine if you must remit the application fee along with your Form 656, Offer in Compromise.

1. **Family Unit Size_____.** Enter the total number of dependents (including yourself and your spouse) listed in Section 1 of Form 433-A, *Collection Information Statement for Wage Earners and Self-Employed Individuals.*

2. **Total Monthly Income _____.** Enter the amount of your total monthly income from Section 9, Line 34 of the Form 433-A, *Collection Information Statement for Wage Earners and Self-Employed Individuals.*

3. Compare the information you entered in items 1 and 2, above, to the monthly Application Fee Income Exception Levels table below. Find the "Family Unit Size" equal to the number you entered in item 1. Next, find the column which represents where you reside (48 Contiguous States, DC …, Hawaii or Alaska). Compare the "Total Income" you entered in item 2 to the number in the row and column that corresponds to your family unit size and residence. *For example, if you reside in one of the 48 contiguous states, and your family unit size from item 1 above is 4, and your total monthly income from item 2 above is $1500, then you are exempt from the fee because your income is less than the $1,667 guideline amount.*

2003-2005 Application Fee Income Exception Levels

Family Unit Size	48 Contiguous States, DC, US Possessions, Residents of Foreign Countries	Hawaii	Alaska
1	$833	$917	$1,000
2	$1,083	$1,250	$1,333
3	$1,333	$1,583	$1,667
4	$1,667	$1,833	$2,000
5	$1,917	$2,167	$2,333
6	$2,167	$2,500	$2,667
7	$2,417	$2,833	$3,000
8	$2,667	$3,083	$3,333
For each additional person, add	$333	$333	$417

SOURCE: *Based on 2002 HHS Poverty Guidelines, Federal Register, Vol. 67, No. 31, February 14, 2002, pp. 6931-6933, increased to account for 5% inflation through 2005, rounded up to the nearest $1,000.*

4. If the total income you entered in item 2 is **more** than the amount shown for your family unit size and residence in the monthly Application Fee Income Exception Levels table above, **you must send the $150 application fee with each OIC you submit.**

   Your check or money order should be made payable to the **"United States Treasury"** and attached to the front of your Form 656, *Offer in Compromise.* **Do not send cash.** Send a separate application fee with each OIC; do not combine it with any other tax payments as this may delay processing of your OIC. Your OIC will be returned to you without further consideration if the application fee is not properly remitted, or if your check is returned for insufficient funds.

5. If the total income you entered in item 2 is **equal to or less than** the amount shown for your family unit size and residence in the table above, do not send the application fee. Sign and date Form 656-A, *Income Certification for Offer in Compromise Application Fee.* **Attach the certification and this worksheet to the front of your Form 656.**

Form 656-A

Income Certification for
Offer in Compromise Application Fee

(For Individual Taxpayer Only)

If you are not required to submit the fee based on your income level, you must complete this form and attach both it and the worksheet to the front of your Form 656.

Your name *(Please print)*

Social security number *(SSN)* **or**
Taxpayer identification number *(TIN)*

Spouse's name *(Please print)*

Social security number *(SSN)* **or**
Taxpayer identification number *(TIN)*

Signature Certification

I certify under penalty of perjury that I am not required to submit an offer in compromise application fee based on my family unit size and income.

Your signature

Date

Spouse's signature *(if submitting a joint offer)*

Date

NOTE: If the Internal Revenue Service determines that you were required to pay a fee, your offer in compromise will be returned without further consideration.

 IRS

Department of the Treasury
Internal Revenue Service

www.irs.gov

Form 656-A (Rev. 7-2004)
Catalog Number 28300X

Appendix B
Payment Plans

Whether you call it an installment agreement, payment agreement, payment option, or a payment plan, the idea is the same—you make payments on the taxes you owe. That sounds like a good deal, but you can save money by paying the full amount you owe as quickly as possible to minimize the interest and penalties you will be charged. For those who cannot resolve their tax debt immediately, an installment agreement can be a reasonable payment option. Installment agreements allow for the full payment of the tax debt in smaller, more manageable amounts.

To be eligible for an installment agreement, you must have filed all required tax returns and paid your estimated tax payments if required. You must also file IRS form 9465, Installment Agreement Request, to formally make your request. The form is fairly straightfoward, but you may have some questions relating to setting up a payment plan nonetheless. This appendix provides some answers to the most frequently asked questions regarding payment plans, as well as a copy of Form 9465 for your review.

How can I save money by paying my taxes?

You can save money by paying the full amount you owe, as quickly as possible, to minimize the interest and penalties you will be charged. Penalties and interest will continue to be charged on the unpaid portion of the debt for the duration of the installment agreement/payment plan. The interest rate on a loan or credit card may be lower than the combination of penalties and interest imposed by the Internal Revenue Code. It is best that you pay as much as possible before entering into an agreement.

EXAMPLE:
If you owe $10,000 in taxes and you are considering entering into an Installment Agreement for 36 months, your payments could be as high as $364 per month, including interest at the current rate of 8% (which changes quarterly) and a failure-to-pay penalty of up to 1% each month. In this situation, you could save $3,102 by paying all of the taxes now rather than entering into an Installment Agreement. An Installment Agreement would cost a total of $13,103 in payments plus a processing fee of between $43 and $105, depending on whether or not the taxpayer is designated by the U.S. Department of Health and Human services to be a low-income earner and depending on whether or not the taxpayer proposes a direct debit payment plan.

How do I set up an installment agreement/payment plan?

If you owe $25,000 or less in combined tax, penalties, and interest, you can use the *Online Payment Agreement* (OPA) or call the number on the bill or notice (have the bill or notice available, along with your Social Security number). A filled-in Form 9465, Request for Installment Agreement, is available online at **www.irs.gov**. This form can be mailed to the address on the bill.

If you owe more than $25,000 in combined tax, penalties, and interest, you may still qualify for an installment agreement, but a Form 433F, Collection Information Statement, may need to be completed. Call the number on the bill or mail the Form 9465, Request for Installment Agreement, and Form 433F to the address on the bill.

You will receive a written notification telling you whether your terms for an installment agreement have been accepted or if they need to be modified.

Are there fees associated with setting up an agreement?

The fees for making an offer in compromise remain at $150. However, the fees for setting up an installment agreement have changed. The fee is now $105 for non-direct debit payment plans and $52 for direct debit payment plans.

If you already have an approved installment agreement from a previous tax debt and your financial situation has changed, you may be able to modify or restructure your installment agreement to include additional amounts owed into one agreement. If an installment agreement is modified, reinstated, or restructured, a $45 user fee may be charged.

Taxpayers who are low-income earners as established by the Department of Health and Human Services can still submit an installment plat for the old fee of $43 regardless of whether or not payments are direct debit payments.

What is the best way to make timely installment payments?

Installment agreement payments can also be made by electronic funds transfer (**www.pay1040.com**), credit card (**www.officialpay ments.com or www.eftps.gov**), personal or business check, money order, cashier's check, certified funds, or cash (cash payments can only be made in person at a local IRS office—do not send cash through the mail). When you arrange for an installment agreement/payment plan, the IRS strongly recommends one of the following options for payment:

- direct debit—electronic transfers from a checking account, or
- payroll deduction—deductions that an employer takes from wages or salary (call 800-829-1040 to set up this option).

These forms of payment help to reduce the burden of mailing the payments, save postage, help ensure timely payments, and decrease the likelihood that your agreement will default. If your agreement defaults, enforced collection action could be taken. Generally, IRS-enforced collection actions (i.e., levy against personal or real property) are not made while an installment agreement request is being considered, or:

- while an agreement is in effect;
- for thirty days after a request for an agreement has been rejected; or,
- for any period while a timely appeal of the rejection or termination is being evaluated by the IRS.

What happens if I miss a payment?

Throughout the term of an installment agreement, your payments must be made on time. If your payments cannot be made due to a change in your financial condition, you should contact the IRS immediately. Failure to make timely payments could default your agreement. A default of your installment agreement may cause the filing of a Notice of Federal Tax Lien and/or an IRS levy action. Either can have a negative effect on your credit standing and cause financial difficulties.

Will a notice of federal tax lien be filed?

The IRS generally may still file a Notice of Federal Tax Lien to secure the government's interest against other creditors. A Notice of Federal Tax Lien attaches to your personal or real property until final payment is made. The notice filing could have a negative impact on your credit rating.

Can I combine other tax balances owed on my new installment agreement?

If you already have an installment agreement from a previous tax debt and your financial situation has changed, you may be able to modify or restructure your installment agreement to include additional amounts owed into one agreement. Additionally, a Collection Information Statement may have to be completed to further illustrate your financial situation. If an installment agreement is modified, reinstated, or restructured, a $45 user fee may be charged.

Will I still get my tax refund?

As a condition of your installment agreement, any refund due to you in a future year will be applied against the amount you owe. Therefore, you may not get all of your refund if you owe certain past-due amounts, such as federal tax, state tax, a student loan, or child support. The IRS will automatically apply the refund to the taxes owed. If the amount of your refund does not take care of the tax debt, then your installment agreement continues until all of the terms are met.

Form **9465** (Rev. November 2005) Department of the Treasury Internal Revenue Service	**Installment Agreement Request** ▶ **If you are filing this form with your tax return, attach it to the front of the return. Otherwise, see instructions.**	OMB No. 1545-0074

Caution: *Do not file this form if you are currently making payments on an installment agreement. Instead, call 1-800-829-1040.
If you are in bankruptcy or we have accepted your offer-in-compromise, see* **Bankruptcy or offer-in-compromise** *on
page 2.*

1	Your first name and initial Last name	**Your social security number**
	If a joint return, spouse's first name and initial Last name	**Spouse's social security number**
	Your current address (number and street). If you have a P.O. box and no home delivery, enter your box number.	Apt. number
	City, town or post office, state, and ZIP code. If a foreign address, enter city, province or state, and country. Follow the country's practice for entering the postal code.	

2 If this address is new since you filed your last tax return, check here . . . . ▶ ☐

3 ( )
Your home phone number   Best time for us to call

4 ( )
Your work phone number   Ext.   Best time for us to call

5 Name of your bank or other financial institution:

Address

City, state, and ZIP code

6 Your employer's name:

Address

City, state, and ZIP code

7 Enter the tax return for which you are making this request (for example, Form 1040) . . . . . . ▶ _____

8 Enter the tax year for which you are making this request (for example, 2005) . . . . ▶

9 Enter the total amount you owe as shown on your tax return (or notice) . . . . | **9** |

10 Enter the amount of any payment you are making with your tax return (or notice). See instructions | **10** |

11 Enter the amount you can pay each month. **Make your payments as large as possible to limit
interest and penalty charges.** The charges will continue until you pay in full . . . . | **11** |

12 Enter the date you want to make your payment each month. **Do not** enter a date later than the 28th ▶

13 If you want to make your payments by electronic funds withdrawal from your checking account, see the instructions and fill in lines 13a
and 13b. This is the most convenient way to make your payments and it will ensure that they are made on time.

▶ **a** Routing number ☐☐☐☐☐☐☐☐☐

▶ **b** Account number ☐☐☐☐☐☐☐☐☐☐☐☐☐☐☐☐☐

I authorize the U.S. Treasury and its designated Financial Agent to initiate a monthly ACH electronic funds withdrawal entry to
the financial institution account indicated for payments of my federal taxes owed, and the financial institution to debit the entry
to this account. This authorization is to remain in full force and effect until I notify the U.S. Treasury Financial Agent to terminate
the authorization. To revoke payment, I must contact the U.S. Treasury Financial Agent at **1-800-829-1040** no later than 7
business days prior to the payment (settlement) date. I also authorize the financial institutions involved in the processing of the
electronic payments of taxes to receive confidential information necessary to answer inquiries and resolve issues related to
the payments.

Your signature	Date	Spouse's signature. If a joint return, **both** must sign.	Date

General Instructions

Section references are to the Internal Revenue Code.

Purpose of Form

Use Form 9465 to request a monthly installment plan if you
cannot pay the full amount you owe shown on your tax
return (or on a notice we sent you). Generally, you can have
up to 60 months to pay. In certain circumstances, you can
have longer to pay or your agreement can be approved for
an amount that is less than the amount of tax you owe. But
before requesting an installment agreement, you should
consider other less costly alternatives, such as a bank loan

or credit card payment. If you have any questions about this
request, call 1-800-829-1040.

If you do not wish to enter into an installment agreement
on Form 9465, the IRS offers alternative payment options.
Some of these options that you may qualify for are:

- 120 day extension to pay, and
- Payroll deduction installment ageement.

For information on these and other methods of payment,
call 1-800-829-1040.

Guaranteed installment agreement. Your request for an
installment agreement cannot be turned down if the tax you
owe is not more than $10,000 and all three of the following
apply.

For Privacy Act and Paperwork Reduction Act Notice, see page 3.   Cat. No. 14842Y   Form **9465** (Rev. 11-2005)

• During the past 5 tax years, you (and your spouse if filing a joint return) have timely filed all income tax returns and paid any income tax due, and have not entered into an installment agreement for payment of income tax.

• The IRS determines that you cannot pay the tax owed in full when it is due and you give the IRS any information needed to make that determination.

• You agree to pay the full amount you owe within 3 years and to comply with the tax laws while the agreement is in effect.

 A Notice of Federal Tax Lien may be filed to protect the government's interests until you pay in full.

Bankruptcy or offer-in-compromise. If you are in bankruptcy or we have accepted your offer-in-compromise, do not file this form. Instead, call 1-800-829-1040 to get the number of your local IRS Insolvency function for bankruptcy or Technical Support function for offer-in-compromise.

What Will You Be Charged

You will be charged a $43 fee if your request is approved. Do not include the fee with this form. After approving your request, we will bill you for the fee with your first payment.

You will also be charged interest and may be charged a late payment penalty on any tax not paid by its due date, even if your request to pay in installments is granted. Interest and any applicable penalties will be charged until the balance is paid in full. To limit interest and penalty charges, file your return on time and pay as much of the tax as possible with your return (or notice).

How Does the Installment Agreement Work

If we approve your request, we will send you a letter. It will tell you how to pay the fee and make your first installment payment. We will usually let you know within 30 days after we receive your request whether it is approved or denied. But if this request is for tax due on a return you filed after March 31, it may take us longer than 30 days to reply.

By approving your request, we agree to let you pay the tax you owe in monthly installments instead of immediately paying the amount in full. All payments received will be applied to your account in the best interests of the United States. In return, you agree to make your monthly payments on time. You also agree to meet all your future tax liabilities. This means that you must have enough withholding or estimated tax payments so that your tax liability for future years is paid in full when you timely file your return. Your request for an installment agreement will be denied if all required tax returns have not been filed. Any refund due you in a future year will be applied against the amount you owe. If your refund is applied to your balance, you are still required to make your regular monthly installment payment.

After we receive each payment, we will send you a letter showing the remaining amount you owe, and the due date and amount of your next payment. But if you choose to have your payments automatically withdrawn from your checking account, you will not receive a letter. Your bank statement is your record of payment. You can also make your payments by credit card. For details on how to pay, see your tax return instructions or visit *www.irs.gov*. We will also send you an annual statement showing the amount you owed at the beginning of the year, all payments made during the year, and the amount you owe at the end of the year.

If you do not make your payments on time or you have an outstanding past-due amount in a future year, you will be in default on your agreement and we may take enforcement

actions, such as a Notice of Federal Tax Lien or an IRS levy, to collect the entire amount you owe. To ensure that your payments are made timely, you should consider making them by electronic funds withdrawal (see the instructions for lines 13a and 13b).

To find out more about the IRS collection process, see Pub. 594, The IRS Collection Process.

Where To File

Attach Form 9465 to the front of your return and send it to the address shown in your tax return booklet. If you have already filed your return or you are filing this form in response to a notice, file Form 9465 by itself with the Internal Revenue Service Center at the address below for the place where you live. No street address is needed.

IF you live in . . .	THEN use this address . . .
Alabama, Delaware, Florida, Georgia, North Carolina, Rhode Island, South Carolina, Virginia	Atlanta, GA 39901
District of Columbia, Maine, Maryland, Massachusetts, New Hampshire, New York, Vermont	Andover, MA 05501
New Jersey, Pennsylvania	Philadelphia, PA 19255
Arkansas, Kansas, Kentucky, Louisiana, Mississippi, Oklahoma, Tennessee, Texas, West Virginia	Austin, TX 73301
Alaska, Arizona, California, Colorado, Hawaii, Idaho, Montana, Nebraska, Nevada, New Mexico, Oregon, South Dakota, Utah, Washington, Wyoming	Fresno, CA 93888
Connecticut, Illinois, Indiana, Iowa, Michigan, Minnesota, Missouri, North Dakota, Ohio, Wisconsin	Kansas City, MO 64999
American Samoa, nonpermanent residents of Guam or the Virgin Islands*, Puerto Rico (or if excluding income under Internal Revenue Code Section 933), dual-status aliens, non-resident aliens, and anyone filing Form 4563.	Philadelphia, PA 19255 USA
All APO and FPO addresses, a foreign country: U.S. citizens and anyone filing Form 2555 or 2555-EZ.	Austin, TX 73301 USA

* Permanent residents of Guam and the Virgin Islands cannot use Form 9465.

Specific Instructions

Line 1

If you are making this request for a joint tax return, show the names and social security numbers (SSNs) in the same order as on your tax return.

Line 9

Enter the total amount you owe as shown on your tax return (or notice).

 If the total amount you owe is more than $25,000 (including any amounts you owe from prior years), complete and attach Form 433-F, Collection Information Statement. You can get Form 433-F by visiting the IRS website at www.irs.gov.

Form 9465 (Rev. 11-2005)   Page **3**

Line 10

Even if you cannot pay the full amount you owe now, you should pay as much as possible to limit penalty and interest charges. If you are filing this form with your tax return, make the payment with your return. For details on how to pay, see your tax return instructions.

If you are filing this form by itself, such as in response to a notice, attach a check or money order payable to the "United States Treasury." Do not send cash. Be sure to include:
- Your name, address, SSN, and daytime phone number.
- The tax year and tax return (for example, "2005 Form 1040") for which you are making this request.

Line 11

You should try to make your payments large enough so that your balance due will be paid off by the due date of your next tax return.

Line 12

You can choose the date your monthly payment is due. This can be on or after the 1st of the month, but no later than the 28th of the month. For example, if your rent or mortgage payment is due on the 1st of the month, you may want to make your installment payments on the 15th. When we approve your request, we will tell you the month and date that your first payment is due.

If we have not replied by the date you chose for your first payment, you can send the first payment to the Internal Revenue Service Center at the address shown on page 2 that applies to you. See the instructions for line 10 above to find out what to write on your payment.

Lines 13a and 13b

 Making your payments by electronic funds withdrawal will help ensure that your payments are made timely and that you are not in default of this agreement.

To pay by electronic funds withdrawal from your checking account at a bank or other financial institution (such as mutual fund, brokerage firm, or credit union), fill in lines 13a and 13b. Check with your financial institution to make sure that an electronic funds withdrawal is allowed and to get the correct routing and account numbers.

Note. We will send you a bill for the first payment and the fee. All other payments will be electronically withdrawn.

Line 13a. The routing number must be nine digits. The first two digits of the routing number must be 01 through 12 or 21 through 32. Use a check to verify the routing numbers. On the sample check on this page, the routing number is 250250025. But if your check is payable through a financial institution different from the one at which you have your checking account, do not use the routing numbers on that check. Instead, contact your financial institution for the correct routing numbers.

Line 13b. The account number can be up to 17 characters (both numbers and letters). Include hyphens but omit spaces and special symbols. Enter the number from left to right and leave any unused boxes blank. On the sample check on this page, the account number is 20202086. Do not include the check number.

 The electronic funds withdrawal from your checking account will not be approved unless you (and your spouse if a joint return) sign Form 9465.

Sample Check—Lines 13a and 13b

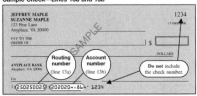

 The routing and account numbers may be in different places on your check.

Privacy Act and Paperwork Reduction Act Notice. Our legal right to ask for the information on this form is sections 6001, 6011, 6012(a), 6109, and 6159 and their regulations. We will use the information to process your request for an installment agreement. The reason we need your name and social security number is to secure proper identification. We require this information to gain access to the tax information in our files and properly respond to your request. If you do not enter the information, we may not be able to process your request.

You are not required to provide the information requested on a form that is subject to the Paperwork Reduction Act unless the form displays a valid OMB control number. Books or records relating to a form or its instructions must be retained as long as their contents may become material in the administration of any Internal Revenue law. Generally, tax returns and return information are confidential, as required by section 6103. However, we may give this information to the Department of Justice for civil and criminal litigation, and to cities, states, and the District of Columbia to carry out their tax laws. We may also disclose this information to other countries under a tax treaty, to federal and state agencies to enforce federal nontax criminal laws, or to federal law enforcement and intelligence agencies to combat terrorism.

The average time and expenses required to complete and file this form will vary depending on individual circumstances. For the estimated averages, see the instructions for your income tax return.

If you have suggestions for making this form simpler, we would be happy to hear from you. See the instructions for your income tax return.

Appendix C

IRS Form 2848, Power of Attorney and Declaration of Representative

This Appendix contains additional information regarding IRS Form 2848, Power of Attorney and Declaration of Representative, as well as a copy of the form and instructions. Use Form 2848 to authorize an individual to represent you before the IRS. The individual you authorize must be a person eligible to practice before the IRS. The eligible individuals are listed in Part II of the instruction pages, Declaration of Representative. Your authorization of a qualifying representative will also allow that individual to receive and inspect your confidential tax information.

The power of attorney authorizes the representative to perform any and all acts you can perform, such as signing consents extending the time to assess tax, recording the interview, or executing waivers agreeing to a tax adjustment. Also, you may authorize your representative to substitute another representative or delegate authority to another representative by adding this authority in the space provided on line 5.

NOTE: *Authorizing someone as your power of attorney does not relieve you of your tax obligations.*

Typically, an unenrolled return preparer is an individual other than an attorney, CPA, enrolled agent, or enrolled actuary who prepares and signs a taxpayer's return as the preparer, or who prepares a return but is not required (by the instructions to the return or regulations) to sign the return. An unenrolled return preparer is permitted to represent you only before customer service representatives, revenue agents, and examination officers, with respect to an examination regarding the return he or she prepared. An unenrolled return preparer cannot:

- represent a taxpayer before other offices of the IRS, such as collection or appeals;
- execute closing agreements;
- extend the statutory period for tax assessments or collection of tax;
- execute waivers;
- execute claims for refund; or,
- receive refund checks.

| Form **2848**
(Rev. March 2004)
Department of the Treasury
Internal Revenue Service | **Power of Attorney**
and Declaration of Representative

▶ Type or print. ▶ See the separate instructions. | OMB No. 1545-0150
For IRS Use Only
Received by:
Name _____
Telephone _____
Function _____
Date ___ / ___ / ___ |

Part I **Power of Attorney**

Caution: *Form 2848 will not be honored for any purpose other than representation before the IRS.*

1 **Taxpayer information.** Taxpayer(s) must sign and date this form on page 2, line 9.

Taxpayer name(s) and address	Social security number(s)	Employer identification number
	Daytime telephone number ( )	Plan number (if applicable)

hereby appoint(s) the following representative(s) as attorney(s)-in-fact:

2 **Representative(s)** must sign and date this form on page 2, Part II.

Name and address	CAF No. .... Telephone No. .... Fax No. .... Check if new: Address ☐ Telephone No. ☐ Fax No. ☐
Name and address	CAF No. .... Telephone No. .... Fax No. .... Check if new: Address ☐ Telephone No. ☐ Fax No. ☐
Name and address	CAF No. .... Telephone No. .... Fax No. .... Check if new: Address ☐ Telephone No. ☐ Fax No. ☐

to represent the taxpayer(s) before the Internal Revenue Service for the following tax matters:

3 **Tax matters**

Type of Tax (Income, Employment, Excise, etc.) or Civil Penalty (see the instructions for line 3)	Tax Form Number (1040, 941, 720, etc.)	Year(s) or Period(s) (see the instructions for line 3)

4 **Specific use not recorded on Centralized Authorization File (CAF).** If the power of attorney is for a specific use not recorded on CAF, check this box. See the instructions for **Line 4. Specific uses not recorded on CAF.** . . . . ▶ ☐

5 **Acts authorized.** The representatives are authorized to receive and inspect confidential tax information and to perform any and all acts that I (we) can perform with respect to the tax matters described on line 3, for example, the authority to sign any agreements, consents, or other documents. The authority does not include the power to receive refund checks (see line 6 below), the power to substitute another representative, the power to sign certain returns, or the power to execute a request for disclosure of tax returns or return information to a third party. See the line 5 instructions for more information.

Exceptions. An unenrolled return preparer cannot sign any document for a taxpayer and may only represent taxpayers in limited situations. See **Unenrolled Return Preparer** on page 2 of the instructions. An enrolled actuary may only represent taxpayers to the extent provided in section 10.3(d) of Circular 230. See the line 5 instructions for restrictions on tax matters partners.

List any specific additions or deletions to the acts otherwise authorized in this power of attorney: ....

----

6 **Receipt of refund checks.** If you want to authorize a representative named on line 2 to receive, **BUT NOT TO ENDORSE OR CASH**, refund checks, initial here _____ and list the name of that representative below.

Name of representative to receive refund check(s) ▶

For Privacy Act and Paperwork Reduction Notice, see page 4 of the instructions.   Cat. No. 11980J   Form **2848** (Rev. 3-2004)

Form 2848 (Rev. 3-2004) Page **2**

7 Notices and communications. Original notices and other written communications will be sent to you and a copy to the first representative listed on line 2.

a If you also want the second representative listed to receive a copy of notices and communications, check this box . . ▶ ☐
b If you do not want any notices or communications sent to your representative(s), check this box . . . . ▶ ☐

8 Retention/revocation of prior power(s) of attorney. The filing of this power of attorney automatically revokes all earlier power(s) of attorney on file with the Internal Revenue Service for the same tax matters and years or periods covered by this document. If you **do not** want to revoke a prior power of attorney, check here. . . . . ▶ ☐
YOU MUST ATTACH A COPY OF ANY POWER OF ATTORNEY YOU WANT TO REMAIN IN EFFECT.

9 Signature of taxpayer(s). If a tax matter concerns a joint return, **both** husband and wife must sign if joint representation is requested, otherwise, see the instructions. If signed by a corporate officer, partner, guardian, tax matters partner, executor, receiver, administrator, or trustee on behalf of the taxpayer, I certify that I have the authority to execute this form on behalf of the taxpayer.

▶ **IF NOT SIGNED AND DATED, THIS POWER OF ATTORNEY WILL BE RETURNED.**

Signature		Date	Title (if applicable)
Print Name	☐☐☐☐☐ PIN Number	Print name of taxpayer from line 1 if other than individual	
Signature		Date	Title (if applicable)
Print Name	☐☐☐☐☐ PIN Number		

Part II **Declaration of Representative**

Caution: *Students with a special order to represent taxpayers in Qualified Low Income Taxpayer Clinics or the Student Tax Clinic Program, see the instructions for Part II.*

Under penalties of perjury, I declare that:

- I am not currently under suspension or disbarment from practice before the Internal Revenue Service;
- I am aware of regulations contained in Treasury Department Circular No. 230 (31 CFR, Part 10), as amended, concerning the practice of attorneys, certified public accountants, enrolled agents, enrolled actuaries, and others;
- I am authorized to represent the taxpayer(s) identified in Part I for the tax matter(s) specified there; and
- I am one of the following:
  a Attorney—a member in good standing of the bar of the highest court of the jurisdiction shown below.
  b Certified Public Accountant—duly qualified to practice as a certified public accountant in the jurisdiction shown below.
  c Enrolled Agent—enrolled as an agent under the requirements of Treasury Department Circular No. 230.
  d Officer—a bona fide officer of the taxpayer's organization.
  e Full-Time Employee—a full-time employee of the taxpayer.
  f Family Member—a member of the taxpayer's immediate family (i.e., spouse, parent, child, brother, or sister).
  g Enrolled Actuary—enrolled as an actuary by the Joint Board for the Enrollment of Actuaries under 29 U.S.C. 1242 (the authority to practice before the Service is limited by section 10.3(d) of Treasury Department Circular No. 230).
  h Unenrolled Return Preparer—the authority to practice before the Internal Revenue Service is limited by Treasury Department Circular No. 230, section 10.7(c)(1)(viii). You must have prepared the return in question and the return must be under examination by the IRS. See **Unenrolled Return Preparer** on page 2 of the instructions.

▶ **IF THIS DECLARATION OF REPRESENTATIVE IS NOT SIGNED AND DATED, THE POWER OF ATTORNEY WILL BE RETURNED.** See the Part II instructions.

Designation—Insert above letter **(a–h)**	Jurisdiction (state) or identification	Signature	Date

Form **2848** (Rev. 3-2004)

Instructions for Form 2848

 Department of the Treasury
Internal Revenue Service

(Rev. March 2004)

Power of Attorney and Declaration of Representative

Section references are to the Internal Revenue Code unless otherwise noted.

General Instructions

What's New

Revocation of an existing power of attorney. The instructions have been revised to allow representatives to use the same procedures as taxpayers for revoking an existing power of attorney. See **Revocation of Power of Attorney/Withdrawal of Representative** on page 2.

Authorization to file Form 2848 electronically. Your representative may be able to file Form 2848 with the IRS electronically. PIN number boxes have been added to the taxpayer's signature section. Entering a PIN number will give your representative authority to file Form 2848 electronically using the PIN number as the electronic signature. You can use any five digits other than all zeros as a PIN number. You may use the same PIN number that you used on other filings with the IRS. See **Where To File** below if completing Form 2848 only for this purpose.

Use of Form 2848 is limited to appointing a representative. If the representative you appoint is not qualified to sign Part II of this form, Form 2848 will not be honored and will be returned to you. As of March 2004, the IRS will no longer treat such invalid forms as authority for the person you named to receive your tax information.

Purpose of Form

Use Form 2848 to authorize an individual to represent you before the IRS. The individual you authorize must be a person eligible to practice before the IRS. The eligible individuals are listed in **Part II**, Declaration of Representative, items **a-h**. You may authorize a student who works in a Qualified Low Income Taxpayer Clinic (QLITC) or Student Tax Clinic Program (STCP) to represent you under a special order issued by the Office of Professional Responsibility. See page 3. Your authorization of a qualifying representative will also allow that individual to receive and inspect your confidential tax information. See the instructions for line 7 on page 4.

Use **Form 8821,** Tax Information Authorization, if you want to authorize an individual or organization to receive or inspect your confidential tax return information, but do not want to authorize the individual or organization to represent you before the IRS.

Use **Form 56,** Notice Concerning Fiduciary Relationship, to notify the IRS of the existence of a fiduciary relationship. A fiduciary (trustee, executor, administrator, receiver, or guardian) stands in the position of a taxpayer and acts as the taxpayer, not as a representative. If a fiduciary wishes to authorize an individual to represent or perform certain acts on behalf of the entity, then a power of attorney must be filed and signed by the fiduciary who is acting in the position of the taxpayer.

Where To File

Generally, mail or fax Form 2848 directly to the IRS. See the **Where To File Chart** below. Exceptions are listed below.
• If Form 2848 is for a specific use, mail or fax it to the office handling the specific matter. For more information on specific use, see the instructions for line 4 on page 3.
• If you complete Form 2848 only for the purpose of electronic signature authorization, **do not** file Form 2848 with the IRS. Instead, give it to your representative, who will retain the document.

Authority Granted

This power of attorney authorizes the representative to perform any and all acts you can perform, such as signing consents extending the time to assess tax, recording the interview, or executing waivers agreeing to a tax adjustment.

Where To File Chart

IF you live in...	THEN use this address...	Fax number*
Alabama, Arkansas, Connecticut, Delaware, District of Columbia, Florida, Georgia, Illinois, Indiana, Kentucky, Louisiana, Maine, Maryland, Massachusetts, Michigan, Mississippi, New Hampshire, New Jersey, New York, North Carolina, Ohio, Pennsylvania, Rhode Island, South Carolina, Tennessee, Vermont, Virginia, or West Virginia	Internal Revenue Service Memphis Accounts Management Center 5333 Getwell Road Stop 8423 Memphis, TN 38118	901-546-4115
Alaska, Arizona, California, Colorado, Hawaii, Idaho, Iowa, Kansas, Minnesota, Missouri, Montana, Nebraska, Nevada, New Mexico, North Dakota, Oklahoma, Oregon, South Dakota, Texas, Utah, Washington, Wisconsin, or Wyoming	Internal Revenue Service Ogden Accounts Management Center 1973 N. Rulon White Blvd. Mail Stop 6737 Ogden, UT 84404	801-620-4249
All APO and FPO addresses, American Samoa, nonpermanent residents of Guam or the Virgin Islands**, Puerto Rico (or if excluding income under Internal Revenue Code section 933), a foreign country: U.S. citizens and those filing Form 2555, 2555-EZ, or 4563.	Internal Revenue Service Philadelphia Accounts Management Center 11601 Roosevelt Blvd. DPSW 312 Philadelphia, PA 19255	215-516-1017

* These numbers may change without notice.
**Permanent residents of Guam should use Department of Taxation, Government of Guam, P.O. Box 23607, GMF, GU 96921; permanent residents of the Virgin Islands should use: V.I. Bureau of Internal Revenue, 9601 Estate Thomas Charlotte Amaile, St. Thomas, V.I. 00802.

Cat. No. 11981U

Also, you may authorize your representative to substitute another representative or delegate authority to another representative by adding this authority in the space provided on line 5. However, authorizing someone as your power of attorney does not relieve you of your tax obligations.

The power to sign tax returns can be granted only in limited situations. See the instructions for line 5 on page 3.

Unenrolled Return Preparer

An unenrolled return preparer is an individual other than an attorney, CPA, enrolled agent, or enrolled actuary who prepares and signs a taxpayer's return as the preparer, or who prepares a return but is not required (by the instructions to the return or regulations) to sign the return.

An unenrolled return preparer is permitted to represent you only before customer service representatives, revenue agents, and examination officers, with respect to an examination regarding the return he or she prepared.

An unenrolled return preparer **cannot:**
* Represent a taxpayer before other offices of the IRS, such as Collection or Appeals. This includes the Automated Collection System (ACS) unit.
* Execute closing agreements.
* Extend the statutory period for tax assessments or collection of tax.
* Execute waivers.
* Execute claims for refund.
* Receive refund checks.

For more information, see Rev. Proc. 81-38, printed as **Pub. 470,** Limited Practice Without Enrollment.

If the unenrolled return preparer does not meet the requirements for limited representation, you may file Form 8821, which will authorize the unenrolled return preparer to inspect and/or receive your taxpayer information, but will not authorize the unenrolled return preparer to represent you. See Form 8821.

Revocation of Power of Attorney/ Withdrawal of Representative

If you want to revoke an existing power of attorney and do not want to name a new representative, or if a representative wants to withdraw from representation, send a copy of the previously executed power of attorney to the IRS, using the **Where To File Chart** on page 1. The copy of the power of attorney must have a current signature of the taxpayer if the taxpayer is revoking, or the representative if the representative is withdrawing, under the original signature on line 9. Write "REVOKE" across the top of Form 2848. If you do not have a copy of the power of attorney you want to revoke or withdraw, send a statement to the IRS. The statement of revocation or withdrawal must indicate that the authority of the power of attorney is revoked, list the tax matters, and must be signed and dated by the taxpayer or representative. If the taxpayer is revoking, list the name and address of each recognized representative whose authority is revoked. If the representative is withdrawing, list the name, TIN, and address (if known) of the taxpayer.

To revoke a specific use power of attorney, send the power of attorney or statement of revocation/withdrawal to the IRS office handling your case, using the above instructions.

Substitute Form 2848

If you want to prepare and use a substitute Form 2848, see **Pub. 1167,** General Rules and Specifications for Substitute Forms and Schedules. If your substitute Form 2848 is approved, the form approval number must be printed in the lower left margin of each substitute Form 2848 you file with the IRS.

Additional Information

Additional information concerning practice before the IRS may be found in:
* **Pub. 216,** Conference and Practice Requirements and
* Treasury Department Circular **No. 230.**

For general information about taxpayer rights, see **Pub. 1,** Your Rights as a Taxpayer.

Specific Instructions

Part I. Power of Attorney

Line 1. Taxpayer Information

Individuals. Enter your name, social security number (SSN), individual taxpayer identification number (ITIN), and/ or employer identification number (EIN), if applicable, and your street address or post office box. **Do not** use your representative's address or post office box for your own. If a joint return is, or will be, filed and you and your spouse are designating the same representative(s), also enter your spouse's name and SSN or ITIN, and your spouse's address if different from yours.

Corporations, partnerships, or associations. Enter the name, EIN, and business address. If this form is being prepared for corporations filing a consolidated tax return (Form 1120), do not attach a list of subsidiaries to this form. Only the parent corporation information is required on line 1. Also, for line 3 only list Form 1120 in the Tax Form Number column. A subsidiary must file its own Form 2848 for returns that must be filed separately from the consolidated return, such as **Form 720,** Quarterly Federal Excise Tax Return, and **Form 941,** Employer's Quarterly Federal Tax Return.

Employee plan. Enter the plan name, EIN of the plan sponsor, three-digit plan number, and business address of the sponsor.

Trust. Enter the name, title, and address of the trustee, and the name and EIN of the trust.

Estate. Enter the name, title, and address of the decedent's executor/personal representative, and the name and identification number of the estate. The identification number for an estate includes both the EIN, if the estate has one, and the decedent's SSN or ITIN.

Line 2. Representative(s)

Enter your representative's full name. Only individuals may be named as representatives. Use the identical full name on all submissions and correspondence. If you want to name more than three representatives, indicate so on this line and attach an additional Form(s) 2848.

Enter the nine-digit CAF number for each representative. If a CAF number has not been assigned, enter "None," and the IRS will issue one directly to your representative. The CAF number is a unique nine-digit identification number (not the SSN, EIN, PTIN, or enrollment card number) that the IRS assigns to representatives. The CAF number is not an indication of authority to practice. The representative should use the assigned CAF number on all future powers of attorney. CAF numbers will not be assigned for employee plans and exempt organizations application requests.

Check the appropriate box to indicate if either the address, telephone number, or fax number is new since a CAF number was assigned.

If the representative is a former employee of the Federal Government, he or she must be aware of the postemployment restrictions contained in 18 U.S.C. 207 and in Treasury Department Circular No. 230, section 10.25. Criminal penalties are provided for violation of the statutory restrictions, and the Office of Professional Responsibility is authorized to take disciplinary action against the practitioner.

Students in QLITCs and the STCP. If the lead attorney or CPA will be listed as a representative, list the lead attorney or CPA first on line 2, then the student on the next line. Also see page 4 for how to complete Part II.

Line 3. Tax Matters

Enter the type of tax, the tax form number, and the year(s) or period(s) in order for the power of attorney to be valid. For example, you may list "Income tax, Form 1040" for calendar year "2003" and "Excise tax, Form 720" for the "1st, 2nd, 3rd, and 4th quarters of 2003." For multiple years, you may list "2001 through (thru or a dash (–)) 2003" for an income tax return; for quarterly returns, list "1st, 2nd, 3rd, and 4th quarters of 2001 through 2002" (or 2nd 2002 – 3rd 2003). For fiscal years, enter the ending year and month, using the YYYYMM format. Do not use a general reference such as "All years," "All periods," or "All taxes." Any power of attorney with a general reference will be returned. Representation can only be granted for the years or periods listed on line 3.

You may list any tax years or periods that have already ended as of the date you sign the power of attorney. However, you may include on a power of attorney only future tax periods that end no later than 3 years after the date the power of attorney is received by the IRS. The 3 future periods are determined starting after December 31 of the year the power of attorney is received by the IRS. You must enter the type of tax, the tax form number, and the future year(s) or period(s). If the matter relates to estate tax, enter the date of the decedent's death instead of the year or period.

If the type of tax, tax form number, or years or periods does not apply to the matter (i.e., representation for a penalty or filing a ruling request or determination), specifically describe the matter to which the power of attorney pertains and enter "Not Applicable" in the appropriate column(s).

Civil penalty representation (including the trust fund recovery penalty). Forms 2848 for civil penalty issues will now be recorded on the CAF. Generally, this applies to non-return related civil penalties, such as the penalty for not meeting the due diligence requirement for return preparers of earned income credit and the penalty for failure to file information returns. For example, Joann prepares Form 2848 authorizing Margaret to represent her before the IRS regarding the penalty for failure to file information returns. Margaret will have authority to represent Joann for all non-return related civil penalties. However, Margaret will not be able to represent Joann for any other tax matters, such as Form 941 or Form 1040 issues unless authorized on Form 2848.

Representation for return related civil penalties, such as the accuracy-related penalty or the failure to file penalty is included when representation is authorized for the related tax return. For example, Diana prepares Form 2848 authorizing Susan to represent Diana for an examination of her 2001 and 2002 Form 1040. If the accuracy-related penalty is proposed by the IRS during the examination, Susan would be authorized to discuss the penalty with the IRS.

How to complete line 3. On line 3, enter "Civil penalties" in the type of tax column and the year(s) to which the penalty applies in the year(s) or period(s) column. Enter "Not Applicable" in the tax form number column. You do not have to enter the specific penalty.

Line 4. Specific Uses Not Recorded on CAF

Generally, the IRS records powers of attorney on the CAF system. However, a power of attorney will not be recorded on the CAF if it does not relate to a specific tax period (except for civil penalties) or if it is for a specific issue. Examples of specific issues include but are not limited to the following:

- Requests for a private letter ruling or technical advice,
- Applications for an EIN,
- Claims filed on **Form 843,** Claim for Refund and Request for Abatement,
- Corporate dissolutions, and
- Requests to change accounting methods or periods.

Check the box on line 4 if the power of attorney is for a use that will not be listed on the CAF. If the box on line 4 is checked, the representative should mail or fax the power of attorney to the IRS office handling the matter. Otherwise, the representative should bring a copy of the power of attorney to each meeting with the IRS.

A specific-use power of attorney will not revoke any prior powers of attorney.

Line 5. Acts Authorized

Use line 5 to modify the acts that your named representative(s) can perform. In the space provided, describe any specific additions or deletions. For example, the representative's authority to substitute another representative or to delegate authority must be specifically stated by you on line 5.

Disclosure of returns to a third party. A representative cannot execute consents that will allow the IRS to disclose your tax return or return information to a third party unless this authority is specifically delegated to the representative on line 5.

Authority to sign your return. Regulations section 1.6012-1(a)(5) permits another person to sign a return for you **only** in the following circumstances:
(a) Disease or injury,
(b) Continuous absence from the United States (including Puerto Rico), for a period of at least 60 days prior to the date required by law for filing the return, or
(c) Specific permission is requested of and granted by the IRS for other good cause.

Authority to sign your income tax return may be granted to **(1)** your representative or **(2)** an agent (a person other than your representative).

Authorizing your representative. Write a statement on line 5 that you are authorizing your representative to sign your income tax return pursuant to Regulations section 1.6012-1(a)(5) by reason of *[enter the specific reason listed under **(a), (b),** or **(c)** under **Authority to sign your return** above].*

Authorizing an agent. To authorize an agent you must do **all four** of the following.
  1. Complete lines 1-3.
  2. Check the box on line 4.
  3. Write the following statement on line 5:
  "This power of attorney is being filed pursuant to Regulations section 1.6012-1(a)(5), which requires a power of attorney to be attached to a return if a return is signed by an agent by reason of *[enter the specific reason listed under **(a), (b),** or **(c)** under **Authority to sign your return** above].* No other acts on behalf of the taxpayer are authorized."
  4. Sign and date the form. See the instructions for line 9 for more information on signatures. The agent **does not** complete Part II of Form 2848.

Tax matters partner. The tax matters partner (TMP) (as defined in section 6231(a)(7)) is authorized to perform various acts on behalf of the partnership. The following are examples of acts performed by the TMP that **cannot** be delegated to the representative:
- Binding nonnotice partners to a settlement agreement under section 6224 and, under certain circumstances,

binding all partners to a settlement agreement under Tax Court Rule 248 and

• Filing a request for administrative adjustment on behalf of the partnership under section 6227.

Line 6. Receipt of Refund Checks

If you want to authorize your representative to receive, but not endorse, refund checks on your behalf, you must initial and enter the name of that person in the space provided. Treasury Department Circular No. 230, section 10.31, prohibits an attorney, CPA, or enrolled agent, any of whom is an income tax return preparer, from endorsing or otherwise negotiating a tax refund check that is not issued to him or her.

Line 7. Notices and Communications

Original notices and other written communications will be sent to you and a copy to the first representative listed. If you check:

• **Box (a).** The original will be sent to you and copies to the first two listed representatives.

• **Box (b).** The original will be sent to you. No copies will be sent to any representatives.

Line 8. Retention/Revocation of Prior Power(s) of Attorney

If there is any existing power(s) of attorney that you **do not** want to revoke, check the box on this line and attach a copy of the power(s) of attorney. The filing of a Form 2848 will **not** revoke any Form 8821 that is in effect.

Line 9. Signature of Taxpayer(s)

Individuals. You must sign and date the power of attorney. If a joint return has been filed and both husband and wife will be represented by the same individual(s), both must sign the power of attorney. However, if a joint return has been filed and the husband and wife will be represented by different individuals, each spouse must execute his or her own power of attorney on a separate Form 2848.

Corporations or associations. An officer having authority to bind the taxpayer must sign.

Partnerships. All partners must sign unless one partner is authorized to act in the name of the partnership. A partner is authorized to act in the name of the partnership if, under state law, the partner has authority to bind the partnership. A copy of such authorization must be attached. For purposes of executing Form 2848, the TMP is authorized to act in the name of the partnership. However, see **Tax matters partner** on page 3. For dissolved partnerships, see Regulations section 601.503(c)(6).

All others. If the taxpayer is a dissolved corporation, decedent, insolvent, or a person for whom or by whom a fiduciary (a trustee, guarantor, receiver, executor, or administrator) has been appointed, see Regulations section 601.503(d).

Part II. Declaration of Representative

The representative(s) you name must sign and date this declaration and enter the designation (i.e., items **a-h**) under which he or she is authorized to practice before the IRS. In addition, the representative(s) must list the following in the "Jurisdiction/Identification" column:

a Attorney — Enter the two-letter abbreviation for the state (e.g., "NY" for New York) in which admitted to practice.

b Certified Public Accountant — Enter the two-letter abbreviation for the state (e.g., "CA" for California) in which licensed to practice.

c Enrolled Agent — Enter the enrollment card number issued by the Office of Professional Responsibility.

d Officer — Enter the title of the officer (e.g., President, Vice President, or Secretary).

e Full-Time Employee — Enter title or position (e.g., Comptroller or Accountant).

f Family Member — Enter the relationship to taxpayer (must be a spouse, parent, child, brother, or sister).

g Enrolled Actuary — Enter the enrollment card number issued by the Joint Board for the Enrollment of Actuaries.

h Unenrolled Return Preparer — Enter the two-letter abbreviation for the state (e.g., "KY" for Kentucky) in which the return was prepared and the year(s) or period(s) of the return(s) you prepared.

Students in QLITCs and the STCP. Complete Part II as follows:

1. In the Designation column, enter "Special Orders."
2. In the Jurisdiction column, enter "QLITC" or "STCP."
3. Sign and date Form 2848. Be sure to attach a copy of the letter from the Office of Professional Responsibility authorizing practice before the IRS.

Any individual may represent an individual or entity before personnel of the IRS when such representation occurs outside the United States. Individuals acting as representatives must sign and date the declaration; leave the Designation and Jurisdiction columns blank. See section 10.7(c)(1)(vii) of Circular 230.

Privacy Act and Paperwork Reduction Act Notice. We ask for the information on this form to carry out the Internal Revenue laws of the United States. Form 2848 is provided by the IRS for your convenience and its use is voluntary. If you choose to designate a representative to act on your behalf, under section 6109, you must disclose your SSN, ITIN, or EIN. The principal purpose of this disclosure is to secure proper identification of the taxpayer. We need this information to gain access to your tax information in our files and properly respond to any request. If you do not disclose this information, the IRS may suspend processing of the power of attorney and may not be able to honor your power of attorney until you provide the number.

We may disclose this information to Department of Justice for civil or criminal litigation. We may also disclose this information to other countries under a tax treaty, or to Federal and state agencies to enforce Federal nontax criminal laws and to combat terrorism. The authority to disclose information to combat terrorism expired on December 31, 2003. Legislation is pending that would reinstate this authority.

You are not required to provide the information requested on a form that is subject to the Paperwork Reduction Act unless the form displays a valid OMB control number. Books or records relating to a form or its instructions must be retained as long as their contents may become material in the administration of any Internal Revenue law.

The time needed to complete and file Form 2848 will vary depending on individual circumstances. The estimated average time is: **Recordkeeping,** 6 min.; **Learning about the law or the form,** 31 min.; **Preparing the form,** 26 min.; **Copying and sending the form to the IRS,** 34 min.

If you have comments concerning the accuracy of these time estimates or suggestions for making Form 2848 simpler, we would be happy to hear from you. You can write to the Tax Products Coordinating Committee, Western Area Distribution Center, Rancho Cordova, CA 95743-0001. **Do not** send Form 2848 to this address. Instead, see the **Where To File Chart** on page 1.

Index

C

D

G

H

I

About the Author

James O. Parker has repeatedly encountered clients who were somewhat bewildered by our country's tax laws, having been a practicing attorney for over twenty-five years. Calling upon his twenty-nine years as an educator at Christian Brothers University in Memphis, Tennessee and being a small business owner himself for over forty years, he set out to take some of the mystery out of the tax code. His first book, *Tax Smarts for Small Business*, was written with the over seven million owners of small businesses in the U.S. who operate through formal business entities in mind. *Tax Power for the Self-Employed* was written to offer tax guidance to self-employed individuals, a group that now exceeds fifteen million in the United States.

A former U.S. Marine and community advocate, Mr. Parker possesses both a Masters of Arts in Economics and a JD from the University of Memphis, as well as an LL.M. from Emory University in Atlanta, Georgia.

A frequent speaker on tax topics, business succession planning, and small business development, he continues to advise others on the importance of tax planning.

Mr. Parker lives with his wife, Linda, in Germantown, Tennessee.